# OUR RED SOX

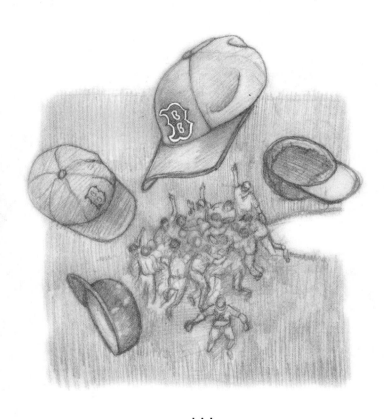

. . .

# OUR RED SOX

. . .

A Story of

Family, Friends, and Fenway

---

ROBERT SULLIVAN

---

books

For further information, contact the publisher at

EMMIS BOOKS
1700 Madison Road
Cincinnati, OH 45206

www.emmisbooks.com

Library of Congress Control Number:
2005920144

*Cover designed and interior illustrations by Glenn Woolf*
*Book designed by Barbara M. Bachman*
*Edited by Mary Bahr*

To Dad—Artie, Papa—

from his kids,

and his kids' kids.

You were there.

# Acknowledgments

DEEPEST THANKS GO TO DAVID WILK WHO BELIEVED IN this book from the first, and leapt into action to make it real. The constantly helpful and intelligent editing of Mary Bahr is also greatly appreciated. Mark Coatney of Time.com first edited some of this material, and for encouraging my Bosox madness, he is thanked. At Emmis Books, thanks go to Richard Hunt, Jack Heffron, Ann Comello, Meg Cannon, Howard Cohen, Katie Parker, Sarah Crabtree, Andrea Kupper, Jessica Yerega, Mary Schuetz, and Amy Fogelson. The speed and surefootedness with which they proceeded: it reminded one of the bygone era of two-hour ballgames. Thanks, ever, to my good friend and former *Flight* partner Glenn Wolff, whose art and design grace the jacket of this book. Thanks, too, to Barbara Bachman, whose equally elegant design graces the pages. And thanks a third time to Wendy Speake, not only for the photograph, but for everything she brings to our household.

The author would like to acknowledge the encouragement given, and dispensation allowed, by colleagues at LIFE, and past ones at both *Time* and *Sports Illustrated.* To the friends mentioned in the many adventures and misadventures in the pages that follow: it was always fun, due to you. Finally, to family back in Massachusetts, and my wife and kids in New York—Luci, Caroline, Jack, Mary Grace—my deepest affection. I love you more than…more than I love the Red Sox.

—*R.S.*

# So This Is How It Feels
. . .

A FOREWORD BY
*Peter Gammons*

HOW WILL IT FEEL? For years we had asked ourselves, "How will it feel if the Red Sox ever win?" How, in God's name, will it feel?

"Warm," my brother Ned had predicted. His relationship with this team dates back to the '30s, and all he knew was that he wouldn't yell or jump up and down or run to a local bar, because it is a private relationship. "It will be a special family matter," Ned said, "and we New Englanders don't share such things with strangers." He thought he would have a glass of champagne, then fall into "a wonderful sleep."

That is almost exactly what Ted Williams had once said he would do at his house in Citrus Hills, Florida. "I'm going to watch the game with some friends," Ted told me in 1986, when last we came so close. "And if we win, we'll raise our glasses and say a toast. Then I'll go to sleep with a warm feeling."

It is helpful, in 2005, to think back to '86; it gives us context for what has finally been achieved, and helps us assess how very good we feel. I returned, recently, to accounts I wrote back then because, well, Robert Sullivan will tell you much about 2004 in his memoir. Let me recall a bit about 1986.

The story was just about as dramatic that year as it was last fall. David Henderson, the Seattle exile whose playoff homer two weeks before against the Angels had saved the day and redeemed so many past sins, broke the 3–3 tie in the sixth game of the World Series against the Mets with a home run at 11:59 p.m., reaching the dugout precisely as the Shea Stadium clock read midnight. It was going to happen, it was absolutely going to happen.

But reality can rarely fulfill expectation, and, after all, we all grew up with the Red Sox' annual tide of hope receding into disappointment and rising back to hope. To relinquish that feeling after sixty-eight years, I remember thinking as I looked at that ominous, witching-hour clock, might be as much of a loss as a victory. Ron Darling, the Mets pitcher who grew up with the Sox, had wondered before the Series began if a Red Sox victory "might not alter the way New Englanders view the world." When Boston's second lead had been lost in the eighth inning of Game Six, the journalist Clark Booth turned to me and said, "Jonathan Edwards, Melville and *Ethan Frome* are part of us, which is why that part of us loves living this ongoing Calvinistic tragedy."

Gary Carter singled with two outs in the tenth, but that still didn't change the burgeoning conviction that the Red Sox were going to do it, they were going to win the World Series. CONGRATULATIONS BOSTON RED SOX momentarily—and mistakenly—flashed on the electronic message board at Shea Stadium as Calvin Schiraldi prepared to pitch to Kevin Mitchell. I thought of the NBC pregame show on which ninety-two-year-old Dick Casey, a chronicler of the 1918 Series, said, "Every day since, I've prayed to God that the Red Sox would win one more World Series before I die, so now I guess I'm going to die soon." Casey was sure, I was sure. Down in the left-field stands, Robert Sullivan and his girlfriend, Luci Rossi— who, in the pages that follow, you will come to know as his wife—they were sure. We were all very, very certain.

Mitchell singled. "They're going to do it," a friend said, nudging me. "Just when we thought that we had been freed at last, they're going to create a way to again break our hearts that goes beyond our wildest imagination. Stephen King wouldn't be what he is today if he'd grown up anywhere else." I thought of the New Haven bar owner who, after the '78 playoff, said, "They killed our fathers, and now the sons of bitches are coming to get us."

And when the ball went through Bill Buckner's legs, forty-one years of Red Sox baseball flashed in front of my eyes. In that one moment, Johnny Pesky held the ball, Joe McCarthy lifted Ellis Kinder in Yankee Stadium, Luis Aparicio fell down rounding third, Bill Lee delivered his Leephus pitch to Tony Perez, Darrell Johnson hit for Jim Willoughby, Don Zimmer chose Bobby Sprowl over Luis Tiant, and Bucky (Bleeping) Dent hit the home run.

How deep does all this run in us? Why is this club—it's just a baseball team, after all—"our" Red Sox. Possessive.

It runs so deep that, on that semi-climactic night in 1986, the late Bart Giamatti, then the newly installed National League president, abandoned his public allegiance and confessed to a feeling of rage. Beside him in the clubhouse, a stranger in a Red Sox cap shouted, "McCarthy, Johnson, Zimmer, and now McNamara. How could he not hit Baylor for Buckner against Orosco with the bases loaded when all Buckner has done is end innings and strand runners in scoring position? Why wasn't Stapleton at first base in the tenth?" After the fan's diatribe came his lament, "What if Roger Clemens doesn't come up with a blister . . . ."

I could feel the wounds opening up again. What if Williams hadn't hurt himself before the '46 Series; what if Larry Barnett had called interference on Ed Armbrister in '75; what if the wind hadn't shifted just before Dent came up in '78 . . . what if . . . what if . . . .

I'm going to travel back another ten years, to January of 1976. *The Boston Herald's* Mike Barnicle, who at the time was with the *Globe,* accompanied me and Booth to the since-razed Abbey Feare. The three of us sat and talked, and watched a Bruins game on the tube. At the end of the bar, an elderly gentleman washed down twenty-five-cent drafts, staring straight ahead for most of the game. When the hockey ended, he turned in our direction.

"How the hell could he have taken out Willoughby?" he mumbled, then passed out on the bar.

In 1986, after the clubhouses had cleared out and emotional exhaustion had set in, the whole thing seemed to make sense. We in New England dwell on history because we are brought up with the English notion that we are what we are is because of who and what came before us. The tenth inning of this sixth game was part of something bizarre and supernatural that was bigger than any of us. "Maybe they are going to win, maybe even Buckner will end up the hero," I told a friend. "But before we could find out what it feels like to win, we have to be made to suffer one last, excruciating time."

"Baseball is not a life and death matter," Barnicle once wrote, "but the Red Sox are."

My very first recollection is of my mother ironing and listening to the 1948 playoff. Just as Sullivan will in the pages to follow, I still vividly recall my first entrance into

Fenway Park. It was June 28, 1952 (Ike Delock, Ray Scarborough, and Dizzy Trout pitched in the 5-1 loss to Washington). When first I went up the ramp to the right of home plate, the green picture and the dank atmosphere gave me the feeling that I had been placed in a forest after a night of warm rain. Sullivan will use a different metaphor about his day in 1960, but I know for a certainty that he felt the same. And so did you.

Sullivan grew up in Chelmsford, Massachusetts. A town that is very nearby, just down the back road maybe fifteen miles, is Groton. At the Groton Elementary School, Opening Day was a legal excuse to leave at ten-thirty, and my father's desk, on which I did my homework, bore the holes of a compass my brother had driven into it in the ninth inning of the seventh game in '46. I listened to Billy Martin's catch in the '52 World Series in the Groton barber's chair of a Red Sox fan named Billy Sambito, whose nephew Joe would pitch for Boston in the 1980s. When I got home from school one May day in 1957, my mother, bless her heart, had written down all the names involved in the Dean Stone-Bob Chakales deal with the Senators. We remember it all; perhaps we remember too much.

I sat in a traffic jam in '67 when someone refused to enter the Sumner Tunnel until Reggie Smith finished his at bat with the bases loaded, and I was in Fenway the night Tony C was beaned. I didn't know, before now, that

Sullivan's uncle had helped to carry Conigliaro out on a stretcher that night. We keep piling this stuff up, all of this stuff about our team. Same year, I found a strong enough radio in my Chapel Hill fraternity to get WTIC in Hartford, just in time to hear Yaz hit the homer off Mike Marshall in the ninth in Detroit (this was after we had already used up a car battery listening to the first six innings of the game).

The last time my brother Ned and I spoke to our father before he died in 1981, he said to us, "The Red Sox will win in your lifetime." Robert Sullivan's father once told him the same thing, and Artie Sullivan was right, too. And Robert's friends in New England who told their children the same— they were right as well. Everyone else said that all of us were crazy, and would be proved crazy. And everyone else was wrong. Our Red Sox did it, and all of us traveled with them each step of the way, with each of our personal journeys a little different than the next. You're about to read an account of one of these journeys—representative, but unique. It's quite a wonderful ride.

"There is no steady unretracing progress in this life;
we do not advance through fixed gradations, and at the
last one pause: through infancy's unconscious spell,
boyhood's thoughtless faith, adolescence' doubt
(the common doom), then skepticism, then disbelief,
resting at last in manhood's pondering repose of If.
But once gone through, we trace the round again;
and are infants, boys, and men, and Ifs eternally. Where
lies the final harbor, whence we unmoor no more?"

—Herman Melville, *Moby-Dick,*
*A Book of Massachusetts—and Mission*

# OUR RED SOX

I RECENTLY LEARNED A NEW DEFINITION OF THE TERM "backpacker." It's not in Webster's and I doubt it will be soon, but as slang it has a certain usefulness—especially in the New World Order.

A friend of mine, Jane, explained it to me. We were talking at a special convening—coven?—of the BLO-HARDS (Benevolent Loyal Order of Honorable and Ancient Red Sox Diehard Sufferers of New York), of whom you will be learning more soon. The conclave had been organized in a rush by club poobah Jim Powers, and publicized on our website by Jim Shea. Powers had been contacted, quickly, in the aftermath of the glorious occasion by the Bosox brass to see if the BLOHARDS would like to gaze upon, pose with, perhaps even touch the championship trophy. This dazzling Waterford glassware was to begin its triumphal procession in Providence on Thursday, and needed to be back in Foxborough to be trotted out at the Pats game by Curt Schilling and Johnny Damon on Sunday night. But Dr. Charles could escort it to Gotham for a Friday p.m. audience if so desired. The BLOHARDS, two hundred strong on this night, so desired. And of course Jane and I, dues-payers since the mid-eighties, were among the congregants.

"Isn't it grand," I said to her as I sipped Jack Daniels in the third-floor ballroom of the Yale Club in midtown Manhattan. Powers had secured the elegant space at the eleventh hour at an extortionate rate. New York would allow BLO-HARDS to gather, but not for free.

"'Tis grand indeed," said Jane. She's a WASP who was raised in Wellesley, but she was into her third red wine, and some deep-in-the-bones Hibernian poetry was surfacing. "I wish Bo could see this."

"How *is* Bo?" I asked about my godson, who had just begun his freshman year at Wake Forest, where he was hoping for a walk-on opportunity with the terrific baseball program there. Bo had attended two or three of the recent post-season games, as had his mom, and he, too, was a true-blue Red Sox devotee.

"He's just great," Jane said. "I drove down to see him last weekend. We had a terrific time. He took me out to the quad at one point and it was totally filled with toilet paper. He told me they 'paper the quad' whenever there's a big win, like against Duke in football. I asked if they'd beaten Duke and he said, 'Mom, this is for the Red Sox.

"'They're backpackers, Mom.'"

A backpacker in this sense is, evidently, a Johnny Come

Lately, a front-runner, a fair-weather fan. Backpackers reside today in Swampscott and Somerville and in Stowe, Vermont, and Rumford, Maine, and Pawtucket, Rhode Island, and West Hartford, Connecticut, and, apparently, in the American South. Bo sneered the explanation to his mother with a proper disdain.

AS FOR ME, I'm feeling rather benevolent about all things Red Sox these days; very hail-fellow-well-met to any and all newcomers to the fold. But I am not, for better and often for worse, a backbacker. Not by a long shot.

I presume I first thought about the Boston Red Sox when I was, oh, a day or two old, still in the nursery at St. Joe's in Lowell, Massachusetts. This would have been in the fall of '53, November, so mine were probably Hot Stove thoughts—trades and such. Farewell Lou Boudreau.

I first wrote about the Bosox when I was five, but I've lost that one, so you are spared. A few years later—maybe I was ten, 1963 or '64—I submitted two pieces of writing, the uberlyrical "First Snow" an an even more accomplished bit of vers libre entitled "Fenway Park," to the poetry editor of *Yankee* magazine ("the magazine of New England," as its slogan says, not, goodness knows, a magazine for Yanks fans). I'm still waiting to hear back from that editor, these four decades later. I think her name was Mildred. I'm pretty sure I enclosed return postage. I recall dropping a loose dime into the envelope.

Not dissuaded in the least by Mildred's unaccountable lack of enthusiasm, I continued to dwell upon (all the time) and write about (often) the Sox. I behaved this way throughout my adolescence, young adulthood, and then into my professional career. This occasionally posed problems. I remember once, a few years ago, I was assigned by *Time* magazine to do a piece on the red-hot Pedro Martinez. I found it difficult to not simply declare our happy headhunter the finest pitcher and finest human being the game had ever beheld. I'm a journalist by trade and training, but when it came to the Bosox I had a bias. One instinct warred with the other.

A few yeas ago, I discovered a path to liberation, a path named Mark Coatney. He's a top (and top-notch) editor at Time.com. He has, for a half-decade now, been an enabler regarding this Bosox condition of mine. Mark has allowed me to wax neurotically, bathetically, psychotically, and pathetically about *affaires du Sox* ranging from my daughter's first ballgame to my dad's feelings about Ted Williams to the Wagnerian ALCS's of the last couple of seasons, not to mention the World Series itself. I write words, Mark runs them—or posts them, or puts 'em up, or whatever it is that web-editors do.

These columns have, over the years, developed their own following among the loyal rooters of the Old Towne Team. The fans send me, via email, their thoughts, their criticisms, their off-season wish lists, their requests for tickets. If any of you are among them, let me apologize here for not emailing back. Some of you seem like vigorous personalities. Some of you, in fact, seem scary.

But I'm pleased that you read my scribblings, and am pleased that most of you enjoy them, or profess to.

These various articles, essays, reports-from-the-field, lamentations, and eulogies have always been, in my view, of a piece. They are part of a great and usually tragicomic personal and cultural history of the Red Sox and us—"us" being me and my family and friends, and the larger us, too: you, them, all of us. The fragments constitute, for me, a Duluoz Legend having the pitcher's mound at Fenway Park as its heart, the sun around which everything revolves, at distances near and far.

In the aftermath of the momentous occurrences of the autumn of '04, I decided to revisit these chapters in the Sox' recent march to greatness and see if I might find the river-run. That was the assignment I made for myself, and I'm sticking to it. The original bits are, however, just bits— pieces of a larger puzzle—and as I dive in, I intend to remember more, and try to grasp the whole of it.

Where to start? Well, it's interesting to me, now, to

reread "Faith of Our Fathers," which went up on the web-site on Tuesday, October 12, 1999. I wrote it from what now feels like another country, one that lies over the mountain and beyond the sea—a place where the Red Sox are not the reigning world champions, and hadn't been for quite some time. It has an attitude and mindset that already, in December of 2004, I am having trouble recalling.

Do you remember what it was like, when we felt like this:

As Abraham Lincoln knew, unique events that happened fourscore-plus years ago provide a useful way of marking time. The summoning of such events, as if at a séance, makes an audience sit up, take notice, realize just how much water has passed beneath the bridge. Also a grander grandeur accrues to the long-past achievement as we reflect on how many human generations have come and gone in the interim—not only how frail is the flesh, but how rare is the deed. Such a bygone event, hearkened, creates nostalgia and longing. That must have been wonderful, to have been in the audience as those forefathers bravely brought forth . . .

The Boston Red Sox last won baseball's world championship fourscore and one years ago, in 1918, and as baseball folk like to say, you can look it up. They did not win in 1919 and, though they came so very close, they did not win in 1946, '48, '49, '67, '72, '75, '78, '86,

'88 and, in this decade, 1990, '95, '96 and '98. This
record can be seen as one of remarkable consistency or
futility—your pick—but it's certainly one that marks the
Red Sox as a companionable second or third banana.
They've been so often near, yet always as far as the
distance between Bill Buckner's feet.

Billy Buck was the first baseman who let a ball slide
past his wickets in '86, as you know, giving the New York
Mets an afterlife, which they ultimately parlayed into a
championship. Buckner's a player in this long psychodra-
ma now, as are Babe Ruth, Joe DiMaggio, Ted
Williams—some great baseball names. But this isn't
about them. It's about Scott, my brother-in-law and the
father of my niece. Scott is not from Massachusetts and
until recently wasn't even much of a baseball fan. His
wife, Gail, my sister, is fiercely from Massachusetts, as
are my brother, Kevin; my father, Dad (or Artie); my
mother, Mom (a.k.a. Lu), and myself. Scott married Gail
and therefore married Massachusetts. He also married
the Red Sox, if he wants to be invited for Thanksgiving.

On Tuesday morning he said to my niece, Callie,
who is fifteen months old, "They just may win it in your
lifetime." Pedro had, the evening previous, pitched six
hitless innings against the Cleveland Indians to cap (as
they say in baseball) a near-miraculous comeback and lift
the Red Sox into the American League Championship

Series against the reviled Yankees. Scott tickled Callie under the chin and said, "They just may win it in your lifetime." They both giggled. Scott was making sport. He thought he was being funny.

When did my own dad first declare, "I hope they win it in my lifetime"? I can't recall. Long time ago. For some few years now I've been telling fellow Sox fans, "I sure hope they win it in my dad's lifetime." They nod knowingly. They either have dads, had dads, or are dads or moms—this applies to moms, too—and no notion can be voiced in New England that gives as immediate and sobering a view of mortality as "I hope the Sox win it in our lifetime." There have already been many lifetimes during which the Red Sox have failed to win it.

It's a painful joke: winning it in our lifetime. Morose. A related joke is that the Red Sox have taken years off our lives. Each spring we warn each other against getting wrapped up in their June successes, as September's swoon or October's shortfall will burden the heart unnecessarily. My mother, for one, tries very hard to stay aloof each year. May, June, July, she will counsel Dad, me, Kevin, and Gail not to care. Dad will have the game on NESN and Mom will emphatically read her mystery novel on the other couch, paying no attention until the final out is made and she can get a "Law and Order" rerun on A&E. August, she'll start to be aware.

This year, by August she knew who Pedro and Nomar were, of course, and by Labor Day she knew that some rookie—"Doobie?" "It's Daubach, Mom"—was having a fine campaign. Shortly thereafter the Sox went into Yankee Stadium near the tail end of a tremendous late-season road trip and swept the reigning world champions three straight, finishing by beating Clemens. I was vacationing on Nantucket with my wife and daughter, listening to the Clemens game on my mother-in-law's 30-year-old transistor radio as Caroline napped in the stroller and Luci shopped the Main Street boutiques. I was telling my sleeping daughter, "Clemens used to be with us. Tremendous arm, but never won a big one for us. He cleaned out his locker once, like a kid taking his ball home, because he was mad at management. Big baby. Big baby's a Yankee now. I'd like to see him fall on his fat . . ."

Anyway, when the Sox nailed the coffin shut that day, pulling within three of the Yanks and sending a shiver back in Manhattan, I called the folks from a pay phone. "I told your father you'd be calling," Mom said in answering the phone. "Isn't it unbelievable!" So she's aboard again, riding with us to whatever it is that fate and the Yankees have in store this time.

Fate. I didn't mean to use that word. I tend not to be fatalistic or superstitious about these things. I don't think the Sox are cursed because they sold Babe Ruth to the

Yankees in 1920, or that the wobbly 1978 home run in a Sox-Yanks one-game playoff by a guy whose name rhymes with lucky was simply meant to be. To believe such hogwash would be dishonor our fathers. What were they believing in, all those years, if it was impossible? Were they idiots?

I'm a father now myself. My father, for his part, is fourscore years plus, hasn't missed a game all season on TV, and has himself in fine post-season shape for this series against the Yanks. My friend John's father, who lives in Providence, is pretty sick, and has us all hoping for his sake that the Sox do it this year. Another John in Andover, Massachusetts (better known as Jake, even better as the Bag), lost both his parents in the past few years, so it didn't happen in their lifetimes. But his wife Annie's mother, in Winchester, is going crazy over Pedro, and Jake and Annie have a son and daughter old enough to appreciate—and share—their parents' excitement. Barry's father, an artist up in Boothbay, Maine, is a fair-weather fan, but it is fair weather these days and he's aboard. Jane's mother in Wellesley told her daughter late last night, during the ritualistic right-after-the-final-out phone call, "I think it may happen in my lifetime." My friend Jim in New Hampshire has a brand-new daughter, and has already assured her that the Sox will do it in her lifetime.

"Pedro," he whispered.

THAT'S HOW I ENDED "Faith of Our Fathers" back in 1999. Hey, can you believe I used the term "idiots"? Spooky.

The Sox did not, of course, get by the Yanks in '99, and John's dad in Providence didn't make it to 2004. Annie's mom did, as did Barry's father, Jane's mother, and all of the assorted kids mentioned above.

Caroline, who was the little one napping in the stroller on Nantucket that early autumn afternoon, was joined in the year 2000 by a sister and brother, Mary Grace and Jack, a.k.a., in our household, "the twins." My wife who was shopping on Nantucket just above (and is perhaps shopping as we speak) is Lucille—Luci—and that completes the immediate family.

Something happened to Caroline in 2001 that affords a good opportunity to tell you a bit more about them all, and where we're all from—geographically, psychically, philosophically, spiritually. Where we are from in those several ways has everything to do with what happened to Caroline that single and signal day at the ballpark. Daddy was trying to do the right thing, you see. Get her started out the right way: psychically, philosophically, spiritually.

I knew precisely how it was going to go; I was, in fact,

going to pre-write the story. It was to be a somewhat clichéd, sometimes sentimental tale of our three-and-a-half-year-old daughter attending her first professional baseball game. During its better moments it would be informed by Donald Hall's *Fathers Playing Catch With Sons* and during its lesser ones by, say, *The Bridges of Madison County*. It was going to be a . . .

Let's not call it an ode . . .

Well, sure, let's call it an ode.

Now, things don't always turn out the way you plan, and life cannot be pre-written.

There was a good deal of back story to the choosing of Caroline's first ballgame, and if you don't mind, I'll lay some of it out here. As with any Family Ritual To Be Handed Down, the elements that made the Ritual rich for the parents, back when their own parents bequeathed the tradition, would need to be replicated for the child. My brother, Kevin, and I were blessed to have in our memory banks the *ne plus ultra* first-game experience, the *Gone With the Wind* of first games. Dad wanted us to see Ted Williams play before he—Ted—retired. The day was fine and fair, the car ride to Boston joyous. Our first-ever trip on the T was a thrill, and then we hastened to the Fens (see what I mean, about the ode?). Three hours in Boston, all pavement and buildings bigger than we had ever seen, affected our eyesight like a dark room, and so when we walked up the tunnel into the brilliant sunshine we were blinded by the field, an impossibly huge and bright emerald with a diamond eye. The Bosox were lousy back then, and this was all for the good, because the sparse crowd made the sounds of the game immediate, hollow. The ball thumped into the mitt and cracked off the bat. I remember leaping to my little feet as the game's first fly ball ascended. Dad knowingly commentated, "Can-a-corn." The out must have traveled all of a hundred feet.

Williams did nothing that day, but who cares? He played, and the hot dog and soda vendors performed admirably. I can't even recall who won. I'm sure the Sox didn't. But, again, who cares? The game was followed by not one but two rides on the Swan Boats in the Public Gardens, then ice cream sundaes at Bailey's, with the chocolate goo dripping from the pewter bowl onto the catchall plate. My brother and I slept on the back couch of the Oldsmobile all the way back to Chelmsford, no doubt dreaming about Teddy Ballgame.

Clearly Daddy—meaning, now, me—had a tall order in attempting to equal that picaresque with Caroline's first game. But that's what Daddies are for, to come up big in the clutch.

I certainly considered Fenway. But the team has been so good in recent years, every game a nuthouse experience, 35,000 jammed in, lungs pushed to overdrive. I felt that the whole megasized Major League show might lead to sensory overload, and Caroline would come away only with memories of shouting and screaming. There could be fist-fights, and with the modern game routinely extending to three-plus hours, nine innings wasn't in prospect. Fenway just didn't feel right to me. I had taken Caroline to the Swan Boats as early as the spring of 2000, but didn't even try to score tickets for that night's Sox game.

Back in the mid-nineties, when Luci and I shared a house with others at the Jersey shore, we had taken in a few Trenton Thunder games. A kid named Garcia-something was playing short for the Sox Double-A club that year, and he was worth watching. The lovely, riverside ball field and the family-friendly feel of the games charmed me. There was a big, stuffed, Double-A quality mascot named Boomer and several Double-A quality contests between innings. I could tell a new science was being applied to minor league games; no doubt this was behind the bushies' upsurge. Good stuff.

So in early 2001 I was talking to my dad over the phone and I happened to mention, "Hey, I see where Lowell has a ball club."

"Oh," he said, "They're all the talk! I never thought it would work, but they built a park down by the Merrimack and it's beautiful. Kevin took me to a game. They painted the Aiken Street Bridge and it looks terrific out beyond the fence. All the games are sold out, even though the baseball's not much."

The Lowell Spinners are the Red Sox Single A short-season affiliate a mere thirty miles from the mother park. They're a team of college grads and muscled-up American Legion heroes in possession of enthusiasm, dreams, and not much chance. Shea Hillenbrand—remember him?—was a Spinner, a fact oft noted in Lowell since Hillenbrand made the bigs. But if you look at what's happened to Hillenbrand after major league pitchers got a glimpse of his free-swinging flaws, you realize that Lowell-to-Boston's not that short a drive after all.

So what? Williams did nothing the day I saw him play, and whether the Spinners were merely bad or really dreadful was of equal inconsequence. The Spinners seemed, to me, the answer to the question about Caroline's first game. As soon as it was convenient to get the family up to Lowell for a weekend when the Spinners were home, I would do so.

Before we get to that weekend, a bit about Lowell.

I wasn't of Lowell, but my parents were. My birth certificate reads Lowell because that's where the hospitals were, Lowell being the city. But I was of Chelmsford, which was thought of back then as a suburb of Lowell, though it is now considered a suburb of Boston. When I was a boy, nobody who worked in Boston lived in Chelmsford, a farm town that was far away. Now, of course, Fidelity white-shirts commute from even farther up Route 3. They come from Nashua in New Hampshire, and every day at six a.m., Route 3's a southbound bottleneck that stretches across the state line.

Chelmsford, still old in some ways, is new in many others. It has had cyber-pervert busts and crazy-person rampages in recent years. A kid who I was friends with in the late 1960s—a real golden boy, a handsome running back on our Chelmsford High team—got upset a few years ago because a psychiatric examiner said he wasn't fit to be a Chelmsford cop. Taking a drastic route toward validating the assessment, Jim Palmer borrowed a gun—from a Chelmsford cop, no less—and killed the shrink and others in her office, then beat it north through New Hampshire before losing his frenzy somewhere in Vermont and, within a snowball's throw of the Canadian border, pulling over and blowing his own brains out. So, Chelmsford's modern enough.

But it still plays Billerica in Thanksgiving morning football, as it has since 1920, and still draws four thousand to the high school field, even when it snows, as it sometimes does, if less regularly than it used to. Chelmsford refuses to hang a stoplight in the center of town and, in a conceit, many Chelmfordians still think they live in the country. As a farm town, though, Chelmsford is very much erstwhile. The only remaining farm that I know of is Parlee's, and I think the Parlees continue to till soil only so their neighbors and friends can pick strawberries each June. The Parlees do it to be friendly, but they're throwbacks. There is no sandlot baseball in Chelmsford anymore, only organized.

So I was of Chelmsford, but then, so was Lowell. Lowell was an idea, an invention. It was, one day, the dustiest part of Chelmsford, then the next day it was City to the Town. Why? Because of a sweet, steep fall in the Merrimack as it rounded a bend upon leaving New Hampshire and heading east for Newburyport, thence the Atlantic. Did you know that tumbling water weighs sixty-four pounds per cubic foot? Well it does, and upon that physical notion Lowell was born in 1821, the first planned industrial city in the United States. The rippling white of the river in East Chelmsford foamed with energy, and energy meant money, and money meant that this 3.5-square mile part of town was going to sever ties with that 22.5-square mile part of town. *Adios, sucker.*

By the 1840s Lowell was the second largest city in New England, after Boston, and the industrial hub of America. Its future was boundless.

*Ahhhhh,* but.

By the time I was growing up in Chelmsford in the 1950s, people from Chelmsford were already feeling sorry for people from Lowell, even though many of the people of Chelmsford were, formerly, people from Lowell themselves, and were, still, people who went to Lowell each day to earn their wage. The Chelmsfordians had escaped a city that had gone into decline further back than any living person could remember. The escapees included my parents.

Lowell thought itself clever in leaving Chelmsford in 1821, but if you look at the record, Lowell has never really been clever. It has never had it figured, not for the long haul. All civics texts tell you to put your eggs in two or three baskets at least, but Lowell has forever put its eggs in the available basket. It came into being only because of that quirky plummet in a quirky river (the Merrimack actually travels east-northeast from Lowell to the sea—an upgoing river—as if it would run over hills to get away from Lowell). Lowell hugged the mills to its bosom as long as it could, then saw no logical answer to their insolent decline when cheap labor in the South doomed the various Athenses and Spartas of the Industrial Revolution. Lowell hung its head and kicked dirt through much of the twentieth century, and then cheered up, moderately, when every town in America was cheering up because we had beaten those rotten Nazis. In the 1950s, my dad, who fought in the War and who worked in Lowell both before enlisting and upon returning, was able to buy a Magnavox console and owned four records: a Sinatra, *The Sound of Music* soundtrack (Broadway version, with Mary Martin), Johnny Mathis's *Open Fire, Two Guitars* (which had a gauzed-lens cover photo of

Mathis posing with two acoustic guitars before a blazing hearth), and *Connie Francis Sings Hollywood Hits* (a particularly egregious version of "High Noon"—"Do not forsake me, ooh my darling. . . "—on this one). Dad didn't have a hundred records and he didn't have a stereo separate from the television. Neither did Lowell. It wasn't a ring-a-ding, rat-pack town—not at all—but my parents did throw an annual New Year's Eve party and the neighbor from Lafayette Terrace always stumbled home drunk. That was worth talking about in Chelmsford. Or, for that matter, in Lowell.

How An Wang came to Lowell I'm not sure, but Mr. Wang was, in the 1970s, the king of the city. Wang Computers represented the new mill industry. Mr. Wang fairly shouted to lowly Lowell, "Put your eggs in my basket." For a while Lowell boomed—a fair use of the word, the town really boomed—and then Wang went bust, or something near bust. I know a lot of folks from Chelmsford, including my mother-in-law, whose final shares of Wang stock turned to scrip.

Lowell's doing okay right now. Wang finally regained some precarious kind of footing, and other, smaller tech firms moved in, one by one, some of them headquartered in Chelmsford or Westford or Tyngsboro. Lowell's trying to figure things out with Asian gangs and other new-millennium affairs that it doesn't have deep experience dealing with. But generally, Lowell's okay. Chelmsford's doing fine, except for the occasional weirdo. The widening of Route 3 is just about complete. All is moderately well in the Merrimack Valley, where a gleaming new ballpark, designed by the firm that designed Camden Yards, sits by a bend in the river and packs them in whenever the Spinners are home.

Which they were that June weekend in 2001 when I drove my family from Westchester County to Lowell for a visit with my mom, who was rehabbing in Lowell from hip-replacement surgery. (That Mom, then 77, was recovering from modern-medical-miracle surgery at old St. Joseph's hospital, renamed HealthSouth or something like that, two blocks from her girlhood home on Mt. Vernon Street, and five blocks from the Jeanne D'Arc Credit Union, where she worked her way up to president during a fifty-year career, still seems to me cosmically significant. Make of it what you will, or nothing at all.) Since we were going up to Lowell to visit Mom, I went online to suss out the Spinners situation. Sure enough, they were home to greet the Staten Island Yankees (Sox-Yanks, what could be better?). I called my friend, Chaz Scoggins, a sportswriter for the *Lowell Sun* and the radio broadcaster of the Spinners games—not to mention the older brother of Kim Scoggins, the quarter-back for whom I sometimes centered at Chelmsford High from 1968 to '70. Chaz pulled some strings. I scored four behind the plate for me, Luci, Caroline, and Caroline's Uncle Kevin.

It was a Friday evening, and we went riding in the minivan down Pawtucket Street past Mt. Vernon, past old St. Joe's (Hi, Mom), past Merrimack Street and down toward the canals, once Lowell's vital arteries, now the center of Lowell's latest revitalization and the site of the ballpark. It was a beautiful evening, the second of summer, humid but sunny. Caroline was napping in her car seat. Luci was back there with her. Kevin, riding shotgun, reminisced about trips to Fenway and the sandlot games of our youth. Papa, as my dad is known to Caroline, had considered taking the fourth ticket, which would have relegated Caroline to Daddy's lap, but finally had said he'd been feeling a little shaky lately and commented, "I don't want to spoil your night by falling down or something. They have stairs there." Papa was eighty-five in the spring of '01, and when a guy's eighty-five you don't twist his arm. He would watch the Sox-Blue Jays on NESN at home, as would Mama in the hospital. (Or maybe Mama would find a "Murder, She Wrote" repeat. It was, after all, only June.)

We drove slowly past the Mill City microbrewery where people filled the patio tables, and pulled into a large parking lot across from the old Wannalancet mills. Spaces were scarce but we found one, and Caroline woke up as if on cue. We locked the van and noticed, over by another old factory, a long line of kids. "That's one odd-looking baseball crowd," I offered.

"The stadium's down that way," said Kevin, who pointed left and then went to investigate, right. He returned with a report. It turned out there was another event tonight, a Green Day concert at the auditorium. Green Day would be a huge deal for the pierced, orange-haired crowd in Lowell. I had, as a teen, seen the Band in that auditorium, and even Dylan's Rolling Thunder Review, but bands like the Stones or the Who would never come to Lowell. These days, no U2. Green Day's about as big as it gets.

Lowell calls itself a city but Kerouac got it right about Lowell in *The Town and the City:* It's still a town. Everyone knows everyone, and everything feels small, even in the shadows of the great old brick mills. This was my personal reflection, anyway, as we walked towards the park. Caroline, waking up slowly, broke my reverie.

"Is Tiger in this?" she asked.

"No, Sweetie. Tiger's sport is golf."

Luci, holding Caroline's other hand as we were in a parking lot (we had from the first day been careful with her, our oldest, our first, while trying never to be overprotective), smiled without laughing, not wanting to embarrass Caroline.

"Pedro?" Caroline asked.

*Single A short-season.* "No, Sweetie. Pedro's in Boston tonight, and can't come. But, yes, Pedro plays baseball. And Pedro's older brother, Ramon, once played baseball with this team. A rehab start."

"I watch baseball with Daddy," said Caroline. This was the mantra in our household: "C'mon and watch baseball with Daddy."

"Yes, Sweetie," I acknowledged. "You watch baseball with Daddy. On TV. Tonight you get to see it live."

"Like *Blues Clues Live?*"

"Just like that."

LeLacheur Park was, clearly, lovely—a sweet little brick 4,700-seat arena placed as softly as a Texas Leaguer at a river bend that had spent a hundred years waiting for a ball field. I headed for Will Call as Luci, drawn as if by a magnet to shopping opportunities, headed for Souvenirs. I joined her after picking up our tickets. Caroline, of course, wanted everything in sight. I vetoed a small bat, which I imagined her using on the infant Jack, and also a souvenir ball, because it was too hard. In consolation she wound up with a bright red bear wearing a Spinners T-shirt.

We walked up the stairs that had scared off Papa, and Caroline, her Bosox cap on backwards, grew more excited with each step. I watched her closely as we emerged at the top and she saw the field, dotted with players. "Ooo-ooh," she said, and looked up at her mother with a big smile. Perfect. I had planned perfectly. Caroline's first game was already a stunning success, a big W for Daddy.

We took our seats, and they were terrific. I think what was at work here was a combination of Chaz Scoggins, whom everyone liked, having great pull in this town, and also visitors from Westchester County, who were a little bit of exotica in Lowell. The Spinners sold out all their tickets before Opening Day, but we guests from strange lands, dignitaries from afar, got to sit a dozen rows up and square behind home. Caroline was rubbing her hands together with the thrill of it all. In the midst of a year that had seen too many hospital visits for and by various members of my near and extended family, I was as happy as I'd been since Christmas.

The Yankees scored. No one chanted, "Yankees Suck!" and, in my estimation, this was a good thing. (I was different when younger, and not a daddy.) The Spinners mounted a comeback in the second, and Caroline and I high-fived each other and cheered on the home team. I glanced out beyond the centerfield fence and saw the old Aiken Street Bridge, painted a rust-colored orange and standing out amidst the leafy trees. It looked even more evocative of this factory town than the painting of it on the cover of my dog-eared copy of Kerouac's *Dr. Sax.* "Dad wasn't kidding," I said to Kevin. "They really have done everything right down here."

Kevin worked for the Post Office in Lowell and was a loyalist. "This has been tremendous for the town," he said. "The Spinners have helped turn things around."

I took some snapshots of Caroline and Luci and then, between innings, Kevin and I went for sausages, pretzels, and Mill City beer. As if to make the evening more perfect than perfection, the concessionaire carded me. I was 47 in the summer of '01. As I left with my licit purchases, I noticed that he carded the next in line, too. This guy looked to be about 60, and I surmised the Spinners must have had some trouble with underage sales, and now had a general policy. Oh well.

As I returned to the seats, I reported to Luci, "Apparently there's a kids' area down there." I pointed to left field. "Games and activities. They say it closes after the top of the seventh, so Caroline should go sooner than later."

Caroline enjoyed a bite of pretzel and Luci had a sip of beer. Then Caroline, who, as I said, was three and a half, and therefore able to hear and understand every little thing, said, "Let's go, Mommy." We were all so happy that night, no reasonable request went unanswered for even a minute. "Okay," said Luci, Caroline slid off her seat. "Daddy, save my place."

"I will, Sweetie."

Kevin and I actually watched a bit of baseball but, due to circumstances about to unfold, I will never be able to fully recall what occurred. I remember a foul ball. It came back directly above the netting, rebounded off the brick facing of the press box, and was heading at the back of a little girl's head when her father deftly nonchalanted it. He handed her the ball and she accepted it unassumingly. I caught the guy's eye and gave an expression that said, "Nice play." He smiled and nodded.

A batter or two or six later, there was another foul. A Spinner or a Yankee—I will never know which, nor be inclined to research it—hit a long drive toward the left-field pole that faded over the short fence. I noticed that this was where the children's play area was, and I said to Kevin, "They're taking shots at Caroline!" He laughed, as did I. I either said to him as a postscript thought, or thought silently to myself, "They should have a net out there."

It was, perhaps, ten minutes later when the hand landed on my shoulder. Usually this meant, "Hey Buddy, could you pass this fiver to the hot dog guy," or if at Yankee Stadium, "Hey, fathead, take that Sox cap off or I'll take it off for ya!" In this instance, I turned and saw a man's face very close to mine, an expression between urgency and fright upon it. I was surprised, above all else. "Come," he said. "It was your daughter that was hit with the foul."

*What foul? What's he talking about? What's he saying?*

Those were the thoughts of the first half-second. The second half of the second was a plunge into a cold pool of water. I was underwater, tingling, moving away from my brother, and swimming up the steps behind this man, the soundtrack of the game turned off, swimming across the top level of the stadium toward left field, floating down steps again and past a uniformed guard who tried to stop me (I couldn't speak and the man who had summoned me said, "It's her father"), past several kids who had been told to stop playing, past kids who were looking and others who were looking away, swimming into a circle of people who were standing around and over my daughter who was crying beyond crying, who was not dead, despite the fact that a hardball had traveled more than three hundred feet in the air and landed with a thud on the right side of her small head, just behind the ear. She spotted me through eyes that were unopened and screamed Daddy. I clutched her left hand. I was not aware of finding Luci, but I was suddenly hugging her on my left side and having my right hand disengaged from Caroline's by someone, an EMT guy, who needed to secure a neck brace and, then, get Caroline into a body brace and onto a flat board that would, shortly, be loaded into an ambulance.

I looked around. Someone was crying hysterically, and I learned later from Luci that this was the woman who was handing out tickets for the rides and activities. Luci had been getting tickets from her when Caroline had been hit. Luci said she had seen Caroline fall. "She went down," was her succinct description, just as you would say of a boxer. I, since I hadn't seen her fall, was forced to imagine it, and even as I stood numbly in the kids' area I pictured Caroline's blues eyes shutting, her knees buckling in unison to the left and her little body sinking to the ground. Her mother had seen this, or something much like it, and then had watched for at least twenty seconds, perhaps thirty, as Caroline lay unconscious.

Since my thinking was incoherent, it involved vague images and weird associations. Caroline going down. Luci screaming (as she did). Cochrane. Conigliaro (whom my late Uncle Fred, once a part-time security guard at Fenway, had helped to carry out that night. Fred told me later he thought Conig was dead). Ray Chapman and Carl Mays and a submarine pitch that no one, least of all Chapman, ever saw. Henry Wiggins, in that last Mark Harris book. *Why don't they have netting out here?* Toes. ("Can you wiggle your toes, Sweetie?" She just cried as she was put in harness.)

Several people would ask me in the next couple of days, "Did they give Caroline the ball?" But at that moment, I wasn't thinking of or looking for the ball. I did look around. Kids at the top of the big rubber slide were standing there, peering down. The ticket-taker continued to cry. Luci was transitioning from panic to her characteristic look-let's-do-the-right-thing-right-now mode, though tears continued. EMTs were everywhere. The ambulance backed into the area. Some Yankee players—their bullpen must have been out in left—came to the fence and looked at Caroline solemnly, which scared me to my soul.

"Okay, honey," I said to Luci, or she said to me. "Who goes in the ambulance? Who drives to the hospital?"

Caroline screamed Mommy, and Daddy. An EMT said Caroline would be taken to Saints Memorial, which I'd never heard of. "Unless you have a preference."

"We're not from here," I said, though I knew that in Lowell there was Lowell General, the old St. Joe's (now Health-something) and Saint John's.

"You don't know how to get there?"

"No."

A Lowell cop appeared and told me that there would be a cruiser in front of the ballpark to escort me to the hospital. "Thanks," I said. And then I had an image encoded in my memory that I will never be able to shake: the sight of my three-and-a-half-year-old daughter, in great pain and shock, being loaded into an ambulance, followed by her mother, also in great pain and shock.

I drifted back to our seats, perhaps accompanied by the good man who came to get me, perhaps not. ("I was sitting near you," he had told Luci after it had happened. "I know where your husband is. I'll go find him.") I hurried past another man and his daughter and heard the father say, "I feel terrible. I tried to catch that ball and nearly did." Our ball? Caroline's ball? He had nearly saved my child.

I usually try to find the sunnier side of things, and as I walked back I had the oddest thought, *She'll be fine. Single A short-season line drive. It's not as if Manny had been rehabbing down here, and had really crushed one.*

I learned something else during this short walk. You absolutely cannot play the game that goes, *If the ball had just been six inches higher it would have missed her, or six inches lower it would have hit her on the shoulder.* Because the follow-up thought is, *If it had been one inch up and to the right, it would have struck her in the temple.* The thought made me shiver, and I nearly fainted. I shook it off and continued toward home plate.

Instincts kicked in. *Always be polite.* Before gathering Kevin and our things, I poked my head in the radio booth to thank Chaz for the tickets. "I've got to run," I said. "My daughter caught that foul." He probably didn't know, yet, what I was talking about. He probably thought my daughter caught a baseball and, therefore, why am I leaving?

The cruiser was waiting for me and as soon as I said, with customary pride, that I was Caroline's Dad, the lights began to flash and we wheeled about in tandem. We crossed the canal and traveled . . . well, I have no idea how far we traveled. A mile, maybe. I do know that as we turned into the Saints Memorial parking lot I realized that this was yet another hospital that had gone under and been reborn. "This used to be Saint John's," I said to Kevin.

"Right," he answered. "I don't know when it changed."

The cops told us to park in an ambulance space, and we took them up on the offer. We sprinted inside just in time to see Caroline, still trussed, wheeled past on a mobile bed and into a room. "Look," Kevin said, not squeamish but trying to consider what was best. "You don't need people here. Let me get out of your way." He went to grab a cab, and though I knew Caroline adored Uncle Kevin and would always want him around, I let him go—not least, because he was right.

Neck X-rays, negative. Head X-rays, negative. Caroline was blubbering throughout, but a trouper. She was coherent, wiggling her toes upon command (everyone commanded it—parents, doctors, nurses). She said, many times, "I want to go home." We tried to reassure her, but what could you say?

Another picture for the memory bank: In a dark room in Lowell, Luci and I, in iron aprons, stand on either side of our first-born child as she holds one of our fingers in each of her little hands and is gently slid backwards into the CAT-scan machine, whose rays begin to dance before her eyes. "Don't talk, Sweetie," I said to her as she moaned. "Just a minute more."

CAT-scan, negative.

"She's had a concussion." I offered this diagnosis to Luci. "I think she's had her first sports concussion." I told her that I got one playing football, that my sister Gail got one skiing. Luci hugged Caroline and rocked back and forth on the edge of the bed. The doctor came to talk with us and confirmed that, in the best of all worlds, this was going to be a concussion, nothing more. "There's no internal bleeding, no break in the bones," he said. "It's amazing, really, that a professionally hit ball could go that far and hit her square and not do more damage."

Professionally hit? I refrained from saying, "Single A short-season," though I did think it—which I took to be a pretty good sign. My real sense of humor, not that macabre mind play I suffered at the ballpark, was returning.

The doors to the room swung open and those two nice EMTs came in, bearing a gift. "The game ball," one explained, and for the first time I thought, *Hey, some kid grabbed the ball that hit my daughter on the head!* That was okay. We now had this game ball signed by the Single A short-season Spinners. A keepsake, even if it was precisely as hard as the one I had denied Caroline at the Souvenirs shop.

"When you get upstairs in the kids' ward, the tiny nurse

about this size is my wife," said the large EMT, gesturing. "She'll take care of you."

"Thanks."

We decided that Luci should return to her mother's in Chelmsford to be with Jack and Mary Grace when they awoke in the morning. I would stay in the hospital with Caroline. We got our room at 1:15 in the morning, and Caroline insisted that I share her bed. It was pediatric-sized, with a firm board at the end, so my legs couldn't hang over; I had to draw them up. For this reason and all the obvious ones, I got no sleep. Caroline slept in fits, waking to vomit occasionally (a usual aftershock of concussions), to tinkle, to cry for Mommy or for Piggie, her constant companion who, unfortunately, was at Grandma's, no doubt equally desolate. Caroline hugged the red Spinners bear as tightly as she could, but it came up short as a substitute.

I watched her all night long for signs of twitching or abnormal breathing, gratefully for her living presence. I said my prayers over and over. Long ago I promised not to pray any more for insubstantial things—a Red Sox win, for instance, even a crucial Red Sox win—but to reserve any entreaties for the truly important stuff. I reflected now, as I gazed at Caroline with a love deeper than that I experienced when she was born, that I'd been doing a lot of asking in the last year, what with all these hospital visits. A lot of thanking, too—and never more fervently than now.

The next day Caroline and I slept and talked and watched TV and slept some more. Mommy came in midmorning, and we wondered to the nurse if Caroline could go home. The neurologist visited and said not yet.

"That nurse, Eileen," I said to Luci. "I think I went to high school with her. I think it's Eileen Ledrew. She once had a date with Mike—Mike Larkin. A drive-in date, as I remember."

"You should ask her," Luci suggested. But I wasn't up for conversation with anyone but Luci or Caroline just yet, and so I didn't ask.

"Go get a change of clothes, honey," said Luci. "Go reassure your dad."

"I will," I said.

Back in Chelmsford, Dad, terrifyingly distressed, expressed the obvious opinion that he was too old for all this, and I offered that I was, too. I told him I had a headache and was going for a jog to clear it. My route when visiting home was a seven-mile loop through West Chelmsford, past the house where I lived until I was seven, then through Nabnasset and back on Dunstable Road to Berkeley Drive. As I jogged I thought a lot of things, most of them lighter rather than darker. She'll never go to another ballgame. She'll never watch baseball with Daddy again. I laughed at the notion.

I jogged along Main Street, an old road dating to

Colonial times where our former house still sits, painted grey now, the house that Dad and Mom bought for twelve grand after the War. As I passed by it I thought, not for the first time, how that used to be an impossible Wiffle ball shot from home plate to the back of the house. I jogged and counted. It's actually only a dozen adult strides. I hadn't been much older than Caroline when we called hitting that wall "a homer."

A minivan passed me and rounded the Dangerous Curve of my youth, which I now realize saw perhaps three cars of traffic per day, back then. The van pulled over. A fit, Marine-looking man got out and crossed the street. I thought he was going to ask for directions, and I figured I might be able to assist him, since I used to be from this town.

"Excuse me," he said as I slowed to a stop. "Are you the dad of the little girl at the Spinners game last night?"

"Yes."

"I'm the deputy police chief from Lowell," he said. "I arranged that escort for you. Did that work out?"

"Wonderfully. Thanks."

"Is your daughter okay?"

"Seems so. Thank God."

"You staying here in Chelmsford? I heard you weren't from here. I heard you were from New York, and figured you came up to see the Staten Island club."

My first thought was that the last thing I would ever do in this wide, wide world is travel to an away game of a New York Yankees affiliate. But all I said was, "We used to be from here. I used to live right down this road, at 148 Main. My folks live on Berkeley Drive now, and I'm staying with them."

"Oh, that's really something," said the cop. "I live down Main a ways, too. I'm Ken Lavallee."

I introduced myself, shook hands, and asked, "Are you related to Leon Lavallee?"

"He was a distant uncle. He worked in the city, at the Jeanne D'Arc Credit Union."

"I know. He was a friend of my mother's. She was president there just before Paul . . . "

"Mayotte," Ken offered. "Paul Mayotte. Sure, I remember her. I remember Mrs. Sullivan. Is she well?"

"Just got her hip replaced. Rehabbing now at St. Joe's, or whatever it's called."

"And your daughter's where?"

"Saints Memorial. We hope to have her out by tonight. My wife's there now."

"Well, we're all praying for her," said Officer Lavallee. "That was quite a thing."

"Sure was. Thanks. 'Bye."

" 'Bye now."

As the van pulled away and I stepped back into my

exhausted trot, I realized that Caroline was of Lowell now in a way that her mother, father, aunts and uncles never could or would be. She was history, like her grandmother. Her grandmother was "Mrs. Sullivan of Jeanne D'Arc." She was the little girl who got whacked at the Spinners game.

The hospital released Caroline that night. Next day, the clan flooded the fourth floor of HealthSouth to finally pay the visit we had come for. Mama, in a wheelchair, was surrounded by her eighty-five-year-old husband, her three kids, her son-in-law and daughter-in-law, and her five grandkids—our three and Gail's two. There was a lot of talk about all the recent trips to the hospital, and about Mom's hip, but the acute focus was on Caroline. She was tired but happy, still with no appetite, and still with an achy neck from either the ball or the brace.

"Do you remember what happened?" Luci asked her at one point.

"No."

"You got hit with the ball."

Caroline considered this, and then asked, "The big one fell off?"

Apparently there had been a large rubber ball at the top of the rubber slide, and Caroline had noticed it as Mommy had reached for the tickets and as the foul ball was descending toward her.

So, then, good. Perfect. Caroline's First Game. We'll never forget it. And she'll never remember it.

AFTER CAROLINE'S HEADACHES had subsided, any number of people urged us to sue, as you might imagine. What professional baseball operation in its right mind would have its play area deep in outfield foul territory, where none of the kids would be watching the action on the field, and not have a protective net up? "Sue their asses," said friends and lawyers, and friends who were lawyers.

But Luci and I had long been agreed that we were not litigious people, and that the culture of complaint in America was a disturbing trend. This was our test case, and we learned this about ourselves for a certainty: We are not litigious people.

Did the Red Sox' ultimate ownership of the Spinners have anything to do with this? Would we have filed for, say, $10 million if the ballgame had been played at the Staten Island park, and the target of our suit was George Steinbrenner's big, fat, left-hand-pitcher-buying wallet?

Those are two interesting questions.

"What I *will* do," I said to Luci, "is go public. I'll write about it." And so I did, first, in an article on Time.com, which was seen by the editor of *Yankee* magazine. He asked for a shorter version for his journal and I gladly complied, hoping to keep the Spinners' feet to the fire. (I refrained from asking if *Yankee* was going to run "Fenway Park" anytime soon.) Finally, much belatedly, a short note came from a team official in Lowell. He wanted us to know that they had put a safety net up in left field. The club theretofore had been reticent in asking anything at all about Caroline's recovery. I was sure they were afraid of a lawsuit, and were being cautious about breathing a word, even to us in confidence, that might later be construed as "on the record." I'm equally sure that if I hadn't taken the story out, there would still be no net in leftfield. People don't do what they don't have to do, and putting up a net would have been an admission that it had been a hazard not to have one in the first place.

As it had been.

As they finally admitted.

So, now, thanks to Caroline, kids are safe at the Spinners' ball park.

The incident did nothing to diminish my, Caroline's, or my dad's or mom's or brother's or sister's ardor for the Bosox (though none of us has yet been back to LeLacheur Park). We supported the parent team through that 2001 season, which of course, along with the rest of the country, suffered the horrific interruption of 9/11.

I am not a New Yorker, but I felt like a New Yorker in

the aftermath of that day. I wrote a series of what-it-feels-like-here pieces for Time.com (this was after the Sox season was well over) and in one of them I commented, "I've been watching the Yankees this week, which has been interesting. My feeling about the Yankees perhaps indicates just how abnormal the world still is here in New York.

Due diligence and full disclosure: I arrived in New York City, for better or worse, on January 2, 1980 and have, all this time—lo these 22 years—fed and nurtured a healthy hatred of the Yankees. I maintained a stolid if stupid dedication to the Red Sox. The Yankees considerable success during my time in New York only fomented a more profound loathing.

It was the fifth game against Oakland when the change occurred, so this proves it didn't come easy. When the Yanks went down two games to naught I might have thought to myself, *That's too bad. They've had a great run.* But that was it. As I recall, the anthrax had started coming in the mail by then, and certainly the bombing had started in Afghanistan. I was busy trying to convince my dear old mother in Massachusetts that Rockefeller Center was a huge place, at least a mile long, and that the Time-Life offices were nowhere near

NBC's. My brother works for the postal service, so Mom had enough to worry about. Anyway, the point I am trying to make is that when the Yankees won Game Three against the A's and then Game Four, I still didn't want them to win the series.

But then, with Game Five, I did. If I remember correctly, it happened around the fourth or fifth inning. By the seventh I desperately wanted them to win it. And, as we know, they did. Then I rooted for them through the whole series against the Mariners. I didn't buy a ball cap or anything, but I rooted for the Yanks, even if I couldn't suck it up enough to cheer for that big lug Clemens. And, today, I'm glad they're in the World Series a fourth straight year, and I'm backing them against the Diamondbacks. Over here, over there, Yankees action everywhere. In the Arizona desert. In the hills outside Kabul. Go Yankees, all.

Next spring, I dearly hope I am a Bosox fan again. If I am not, the world is still on its head, and New York is still in bad, bad shape.

Well, my friends back home—Mike, Barry, Bruce, the Bag—all got in touch pronto after that one was posted, wondering if I was, in fact, okay. I assured them I was as okay as was possible, more okay than most New Yorkers.

As for the next spring, clearly the world was still on its head, but I was a Sox fan again. How long could I not have been?

But also, that spring, our personal crucible.

I LOVED—AND LOVE—my dad, Boston, Ted, and the Red Sox in just about that order. In the spring of 2002, everything came into confluence.

At the time I was feeling extremely warm not towards Pedro and Nomar & Co., but towards Tom Brady and Drew Bledsoe. While I had never, 9/11 excepted, wavered in my devotion to, principally, the Bosox, there were always the Pats, second, with the Celts third, and then the Bruins. In '01, when that particularly ugly Red Sox team had come apart like an old Rawlings in early autumn, it was hard on my dad, who was then eighty-five.

The Pats, by contrast, gave us something to talk about, week in and week out, all that autumn and winter. Here was an overachieving collective with a classy vet and a young lion and, well, it was all you could have hoped for in a sports team. I am in this journalism racket and, therefore, I can usually score tickets or credentials (I'm not rubbing it in, I'm just saying). But I didn't chase opportunities to see the Patsies play in that post-season. I was content to sit before the tube, suck down a Sam Adams, and call Artie every quarter on the quarter to compare notes. I was not at the Snow Bowl or the Super Bowl, but I was there with my dad. Luci, Caroline, and the twins were asleep, and I was alone by the tube on those two late nights, even the Super one. I was alone, but hardly alone. I was with Dad. Mom was hopelessly asleep in Chelmsford, and so Dad and I would sit with our cell phones on our laps and watch the action.

"How about that!"

"In the snow!"

*"Jee-zus!"*

"Bledsoe!"

"Brady's really something!"

Those are excerpts.

After the season, Dad clipped a full-page ad that Bledsoe had placed in the *Globe* and mailed it to me. In the advertisement, Bledsoe thanked the fans of New England for all their support, and said he would never forget them, even as he led Buffalo into whatever future awaited. Dad's scribbled note read: "Always a classy guy." That was the key thing for Dad. Such as Bledsoe, Plunkett, and Parilli; Nomar, Tiant, and Lonborg; Bird, Cousy, and Russell; Bourque, Bucyk, and Orr: classy guys. The Carl Everetts and Terry Glenns of the world he had little use for, even if they wore our uniforms. He got a kick out of the Spacemen and Oil Cans, but it was the classy guys he defended.

Ted Williams was, of course, a classy guy, perhaps the classiest. "You know how much money he raised for the little kids with cancer?" Dad would ask me if I teased him about the Kid spitting at fans. "Millions. You know how many wars he fought in? Two. Two wars, and he really fought. A Marine. None of that USO stuff. And don't talk to me about him and the sportswriters. You know that sportswriter, Shaughnessy? Ted found out that Shaughnessy's little girl was sick. He called the girl up from Florida. A classy guy."

Growing up when Dad did and where he did, marrying when he did and having kids when he did, of course he took my brother and me to that ballgame at Fenway before Ted Williams retired. He had no choice.

It's one of the great memories of my life. I was six and Kevin was eight in that summer of 1960 when Dad drove us down Route 3, then onto what he considered the terrifying Route 2, thence to the even more harrowing Storrow Drive and a backstreet parking space that wasn't tough to find since not more than seven or eight or ten thousand fans were there that day, Teddy Ballgame's twilight notwithstanding.

As implied earlier, this was nothing about baseball—well, next to nothing—but all about tradition and legacies: beans, cod, Boston, the Bosox. "You've got to see this guy play," Dad had said. "He won't be playing much longer."

With that game in 1960 Dad secured something for himself, too. He saw Williams play in each of four decades. He had caught Ted coming up as a brash phenom in '39. Then both men had gone off to the War. Then Dad had gotten a GI Bill deal after his discharge to attend Suffolk Law at night while working in Lowell days. Back then you could go to law school without ever landing a B.A., and the postwar rules were that you had to be *ed-u-cated*. So Dad found these night courses at Suffolk, though he never intended to be a lawyer, and he would drive to Boston after work in pursuit of his L.L.D, while Mom, who had loved him since 1938 but had waited until the hostilities were over—they're romantic, but prudent, in Lowell—enrolled in Fanny Farmer's cooking school so that she could keep Artie company each evening in the Mercury. The year was 1946 and because of what the Splendid Splinter was up to, Artie and Lu didn't log a lot of class time. They would park the car, hasten to the Fens (is that the second time I've used that?) and take in the Sox game. The ex-Army sergeant would drive Route 3 each evening with his soon-to-be fiancée, then would cut class to watch the ex-Marine fighter pilot lead a rare and wonderful Red Sox team to the pennant, if not to the championship.

The family joke would long be that their courtship was carried out largely in the presence of Ted Williams. Perhaps it was all for the good. Their kids turned out to be pretty fair at cramming for tests, too, and would of course become diehard Bosox fans in the measure, which we now know to be a very good thing indeed. Yes, in this time of glorious deliverance for diehard Bosox fans, we can finally consider that a good thing.

Dad's intense loyalty to Williams must have dated to that magic summer of '46, when Lu and Artie fell ever more deeply in love. Life must have looked just about perfect to Artie that summer, and Ted Williams must have looked like perfection personified. The noted nature writer Bob Boyle once told me, "I'm not amazed that the greatest hitter who ever lived was such a good fisherman, I'm amazed that the greatest game fisherman who ever lived could hit a curveball 500 feet!" That's how good Williams was. The day Boyle told me that, I couldn't wait to call Dad and share the reflection.

Perfection. And Dad used this perfect, imperfect man to introduce us to the Red Sox. Yes, Ted did nothing on the day my dad took Kevin and me to see him play. Oh-for-something, maybe a couple of putouts in left, but, in sum, zippo. Still, Dad had done his job. He had got us started.

My father, as I'm sure you've inferred, died in that spring of 2002. It came pretty quickly—too quickly for the family—as lung cancer claimed him at eighty-six. My mom, sister, brother, and I had noticed him getting skinnier, but we had probably been in the same denial that he had exercised before receiving the X-Ray results from the Lahey Clinic that May. At the time we were told he had six months to live if he did nothing. He was too old for surgery or chemo, but radiation might help. We started researching like mad and learned about a new drug that made things more comfortable for, and perhaps even shrank tumors in, elderly lung cancer patients. We found a doctor at Lahey who was one of those prescribing the drug. The physician confirmed to me that Dad might be a proper candidate. But by then Dad was scheduled for several weeks of radiation, and it was decided to finish that, then see.

Dad, a two-pack-a-day guy since before the War, had done everything he could to fight mortality in his later years, including giving up cigarettes in the early '90s after a mild stroke. You see, his kids had married late and, therefore, his five grandchildren had come into his life late. He loved them dearly and wanted to see them grow a bit. He wanted to see them throw and catch a baseball. As Christmas 2001 turned into the spring of 2002, he wanted one more summer. He was sure the older cousins, (our Caroline, and Scott and Gail's Callie) would be swimming in the deep end by September. That he wanted to see. He sent three pair of his best short pants to the tailor and had the waist taken in on each. He was getting ready for the hot weather.

It was not to be. The radiation knocked the stuffing out

of him. I sensed this a bit when last I saw him, in Massachusetts, that Memorial Day weekend. My mom and siblings were seeing him every day and so changes weren't as apparent to them. But as we sat in chairs on the lawn of my sister's place in Wellesley, sipping drinks and watching the kids play, the Sox game on the radio and discussion continually circling around to how well they were doing that year, Dad looked frail. My sister and I talked about discussing a switch in protocols with Artie's radiation doc—maybe that drug's an answer?—and, then, Artie plunged into four tough days and was dead. Suddenly. Just like that. A bolt to our consciousness. My brother wound up in the hospital himself with a bleeding ulcer, and the rest of us wound up bereft. (As is always the case with most all families, I do realize.)

Just before Dad died I had attended the semi-annual gathering of the BLOHARDS in New York City held before the first Yankee Stadium Bosox-Yanks game of the year (won by us, by the way). I hung out for a while with the Sox broadcaster Jerry Trupiano, met the young reserve second baseman Bryant Nelson, and, then, enjoyed the company of my tablemate, Bill Nowlin, and his son. Bill is the founder and head honcho of Rounder Records in Cambridge and a Red Sox lunatic of the first water, not to mention a Ted Williams fanatic. He knew the Kid, actually knew him. Nowlin had visited Ted in Florida in the waning weeks of 2001, and had then contributed a very good piece to the *Globe Sunday Magazine* about Williams' Spanish heritage.

I asked Nowlin how Ted was doing and, only then, realized that Ted and my dad were in the same straits. Nowlin said Williams had had heart surgery in early 2001 and had been, essentially, day-to-day ever since.

"What's Williams like?"

"Oh, he's terrific," Nowlin said.

"A classy guy?"

"Absolutely."

I was glad to hear it. I thought back to when DiMaggio had died and, then, the Richard Ben Cramer bio had come out indicating that Jolting Joe had been sorely lacking in the humanity department—quite a contrast from Cramer's "What Do You Think Of Ted Williams Now?"

"How about that," Dad had said during a discussion of the matter, "our fella was classier than their fella after all."

"Our fella spit at the fans," I said, teasing.

When someone whom you know dies, you learn some secrets. Even if you figured you knew everything, there are secrets. "Artie was very proud of that," my brother told me about Dad's war service. This happened during the week of the funeral in Chelmsford.

"Really?"

"Absolutely."

He had been a Master Sergeant in the Army, assigned to regiments that tailed the first wave on D-Day and into the Bulge. He had done well, I always assumed, but I assumed further that it hadn't meant much to a guy who was extremely modest and unforthcoming about himself. I knew he had been awarded the Bronze Star, but the medal had been lost in a house fire back in the late 1950s and he had never sought a replacement through the Veterans Administration. So, I figured, how much could it have meant to him?

As I've said, well before Ted Williams became a lovable figure in our region, my dad defended him. I assume now that this had something to do with their shared duty in World War II. I'll never know. What I do know is that much of Boston reviled the Splinter for much of his and my lifetime, but in our family, Ted was not to be reviled. Dad felt or sensed that Ted had the critical things—the things having to do with class—in proper order. And so he deserved our support.

And so did the Red Sox generally, even if they were, in those later Williams Years, thoroughgoing losers. So many memories of those times, no matter how bad the baseball. I remember Dad leaning close to the radio one evening when Kevin and I came back from fishing down by the Red House—a small power station for the dam on Stony Brook in West Chelmsford. Earl Wilson was finishing his no-hitter, a two-nothing job that he had to win by himself with a homer because the Sox were such poor batsmen. "Listen to this," Dad said as we came in through the screen door (which slammed shut after allowing, oh, only a hundred or so mosquitoes to pass). "It's the eighth and Wilson hasn't given up . . ." He caught himself, not wanting to jinx anything.

We did get treated to that occasional sporting thrill, even in the leanest years. Not only Wilson, who was a good pitcher, after all, but also Monbo and even—goodness!—Morehead tossed hitless games. Malzone was a solid third-baseman, and (Three-and-two-to) Eddie Bressoud, while no Pesky, wasn't a bad shortstop. And then, of course, there was my generation's hero: Yaz. If he was not Ted, he was the next best thing. If we had had a few more ballplayers like the guys who patrolled left for us through much of the twentieth century—Williams, Yaz, Rice—we'd have won our share. If If If.

One day we woke up and Yastrtzemski had been joined on the club by a starting pitcher who really looked like a starting pitcher, a tall and handsome guy named Lonborg. I remember August and September of 1967 as if they were yesterday, those two men—Yaz and Lonborg—lugging, positively *lugging* a team that, besides its two stars, looked like your stadard issue Red Sox. They lugged them all the way to the pennant, then all the way to Game Seven against the Cards. Gibson had three days' rest and our Gentleman Jim only two, so what can you do? "They came close," Dad said simply. I did the math and realized Dad hadn't seen them come that close since the summer of '46, twenty-one years.

The several seasons after the Impossible Dream were funny ones, sometimes even ha-ha funny. Remember the Hawk Harrelson Years? Red Sox history is cluttered—littered?—with some pretty strange mini-epochs, if only a few of them went into the evening snapping their fingers and dressed in Nehru jackets. "He's a character," Dad said. Artie Sullivan voted Democrat most of his life, but was a modest, conservative guy. I was surprised to detect a hint of admiration in his voice. "He's a free swinger, that Hawk." Dad was pleased with his clever double-meaning.

I remember '75 and '78 vividly, of course. Dad came home from work the day after the Fisk home run and said that his secretary, a woman of mature years, had greeted him in the bank parking lot with a hug—"she practically jumped into my arms. Nearly knocked me over"—and had shouted, "How about that, Arthur!" Great years, '75 and '78, great years—right till their bitter ends.

I remember the big games, but also the small ones. I remember a game in the early '80s when Dad and I were finally in role-reversal: *I* took *him* to Fenway. It was a midweek afternoon game in April, back in the days—not so long ago—when the Sox wouldn't schedule a night game until a little later in the season, when New England warmed up a bit. Anyway, on this particular Tuesday or Wednesday, electrical power had been knocked out in Kenmore Square and, therefore, throughout Fenway Park. The ballgame that day was all round sounds and cheers—bat on ball, *"Steeeerike One!"* "Getcha peanuts!" "Na battah, no battah!" It sounded quite like that first game that Dad had taken Kevin and me to see, the Ted game with the near-empty stadium. It was wonderful, magical. I was probably twenty-seven or twenty-eight years old and had just landed an entry-level edit job with *Sports Illustrated*. I subsequently wrote an account of the special day and submitted it to the editor of our Scorecard section—the short bits up front. The editor was kind enough to run it, and awarded me what was known as an "interior byline."

Not so terribly long ago, when I was back home for a visit, Mom gave me something that she had found in Dad's very small pile of saved possessions. It was a blown-up, framed version of the Scorecard item, headlined "Power Failure." "You'll want this," she told me. "This is when you took Artie to Fenway for his birthday." I hadn't remembered it had been his birthday. I read it silently:

A fire at a Boston Edison substation last
Wednesday afternoon left Fenway Park without

electric power during the Red Sox' 7-2 win over Baltimore before 8,925 shivering fans. Because of the power failure, there were no lights in the public restrooms, and some players griped that the clubhouses were too icy for them to get properly warmed up, but one spectator, *SI* reporter Robert Sullivan, had no complaints. Sullivan found that along with Fenway's other renowned charms—cozy dimensions, real grass, etc.—the absence of electricity helped evoke the image of "what baseball must have been like circa 1905." He reports:

Whenever you pass through Fenway's brick portals on a bright, sunny day, you're immediately struck by how dark it is under the stands. This day it takes a particularly long time for the eyes to adjust. No lights are on, no public-address announcements are heard, and the clocks that should indicate five minutes till game time aren't working. It is left to P.A. announcer Sherm Feller to open a press-box window, poke his head out, and, with a bullhorn, call out the starting lineups. The words are barely audible to the umpires and managers gathered at home plate, who laughingly ask Feller to speak up. Without John Kiley's electric organ to get things going, Feller now must assume another chore. "I'm going to start this off in a logical key," he shouts. "Ohhhh, say can you

see . . ." The national anthem gets off to a shaky
start, but soon the crowd takes up the tune. It's a
soft, oddly stirring rendition. At the end the
applause is vigorous.

With the electronic message board in center
blackened, the scoreboard in left, the only one in
the American League still set by hand, takes on
attention-riveting importance. But communication
with the press box is uncertain. While the four runs
the Red Sox score in the first inning are duly
recorded, the Oriole run in the second is ignored.
Word is passed along to the scoreboard operators
about the missing run, and it's finally posted—for
Boston, making it, erroneously, 5-0. An emissary
jogs across the leftfield grass to advise of the mistake, and by the top of the next inning, the O's
finally are credited with their run.

Some fans learn how to keep score this afternoon; if you already know how, you're enlisted to
tutor. In the absence of the usual drumbeat of
amplified information, people seem to pay closer
attention to the action on the field. Not a hit or a
good play is missed. Despite the cold, most of the
crowd remains until the end of the well-played
game, during which there have been not only no
P.A. announcements or organ music, but also no

larger-than-life instant replays or cheery greetings to visiting school and civic groups. All in all, a chilly early-season afternoon at the ball park to be cherished.

With a blue felt-tip pen I had, twenty-three years ago, written at the bottom, "To Dad—Your birthday . . . Our Game. April '82 about April '81. Love, Bob."

I read the Scorecard item to myself, but in mom's presence, and was amazed, frankly, that I was able to hold back tears. The framed account now hangs in our garage in Westchester, on the wall that includes my boyhood Red Sox pennant, the old *SI* with Ted on the cover (hitting tips inside!), an ad for Chesterfields, featuring both Ted and Stan the Man, and another boosting Ted's Root Beer. And, now, a framed cover of *Time,* Keith Foulke in Jason Varitek"s arms, cover-copy reading, "The Joy of Sox"—a present, Christmas of '04, from Jane and Steve. *We got it done Dad.*

I'm trying to remember, just now, what that visit to Chelmsford was about. Maybe to help Mom clean out some things. My family has been going back up there a lot in the last few years—as often as we can to see Luci's mom, mine, Kevin, Gail, Scott, and the kids.

And perhaps we go because we regret not getting up there more frequently in Dad's last months.

Luci and I first had that discussion about getting in the car and pointing it north "just because" as we were approaching the Fourth of July weekend in that summer of '02. Sure, there were things going on at the pool in Westchester . . . And sure, there was a birthday party that Caroline was invited to . . . And sure, there was . . .

"Let's just go. Just because."

It was funny being up there, at that particular time—a time that those of you among the fanship who know all the stats—years of service, OBP, fielding percentage, birth dates, death dates, that sort of arcana—probably have already registered. It surprised me not at all when I learned on that Friday that Ted Williams had died. "Makes sense we're up in Beantown," I said to my sister as we sipped Sam Adams in Wellesley. "I can't believe, though, what's happened since Dad died. Rosie Clooney with the lung cancer. Now Ted Williams. Dad's favorites."

My sister had earlier expressed the opinion that if the Red Sox did win it all that year, she would hate them forever since Artie would miss it. But now we joked with one another. Let's say that all of our younger notions of faith were correct, I suggested. Let's assume that the way we envisioned the hereafter, back when faith could be taken on faith, was precisely the way it was. Then, certainly, in the precinct of heaven reserved for Boston-centric, war veteran Bosox fanatics, two recent arrivals, Dad and Ted, were looking down, watching the action. Ted would certainly have enough bravado to approach Babe Ruth and tell him to cut the crap with this Curse of the Bambino stuff. "Maybe if they win it this year," Gail suggested finally, "it's actually because Dad's up there. Dad and Ted."

Yeah, maybe.

But the facts are, the Bosox played like dogs that weekend and lost twice to Detroit.

To reiterate: Detroit.

Maybe Ted was having trouble getting by St. Peter. After all, he did spit at the fans. His favorite adjective, constantly deployed during waking hours, was "goddamned." He used far, far more vulgar words nearly as frequently.

I can see Dad wandering out to the Pearly Gate, shambling up to St. Pete: "You know how much he raised for the kids with cancer? Millions. You know how many wars. . ."

"There are a few things I wish Dad hadn't lived to see," I said to my sister on the Sunday of our visit. "I wish he hadn't seen Caroline get whacked a year ago. I wish he hadn't seen September 11th. I wish he hadn't seen the church scandal.

"I guess I'm glad he didn't see Ted Williams die. That would have made him feel even older."

We were on our way to church when I shared that notion. My sister's parish in Wellesley is St. John the Evangelist, the famous one where the laity rose up to challenge

Cardinal Law, where Voice of the Faithful was founded. That is and isn't beside the point. Dad was pleased that Gail attended a church that saw things clearly. And he would have appreciated a priest who was not shy about beginning his homily with words concerning Ted Williams.

The sermon was about perfection—apparent perfection versus the real thing—and after applauding Williams not only for his .344 lifetime average and his service in two wars but for his tireless work on behalf of kids with cancer, the subject quickly became Jesus. In Greater Boston that weekend, this was no great journey from Teddy Ballgame to Christ. It was a perfectly sensible segue, a New England metaphor that the congregation easily understood and fully appreciated. There were smiles throughout the church, and knowing nods.

"Who died?" Caroline asked me on our way to the parking lot. She was still so young, only four, and had just had a month of learning far too much about death.

"Ted Williams. He was a baseball player."

"With a B-hat?"

"Yes. He was the best B-hat player ever."

"Did he know Papa?"

"No. But Papa knew him."

"Maybe he'll meet Papa now."

"I certainly hope so," I said as I gave my daughter a hug. "He'd like Papa."

Back at Gail's house we packed quickly, hoping to beat the Mass Pike traffic on our way home. "We'll be back soon," I said as I gave my sister a little kiss. "We've decided we'll be coming north more often."

NORTH.

I'm forever driving north in these stories. What's that about, besides the obvious (if I want to sit in Fenway, I must go north)? Going home or, perhaps, trying to escape?

Certainly since Dad died, it has been about going home. And certainly, too, there is always, for a Red Sox fan in the New York sphere of influence, a strong element of escape.

And what is that like, you might ask, living as an enemy behind enemy lines? Well . . .

It's *interesting*.

It's not always dangerous.

But it is interesting, on a near-constant basis.

I'll tell you what it's like for us—my family—and also about a larger family, the BLOHARDS, whom we've glancingly met earlier. I'll tell you what life is like for those from the north who live—and raise their children—further south.

By now we have reached, in our meander, late March of

2003. Spring was—at last—in the air. The snowmelt was gaily gushing into its cozy reservoir in our cellar, and after a winter that really had been a winter, even by New England standards, we Westchesterites were finally skipping merrily about in cotton sweaters. There were nearly as many towhees as squirrels at the birdfeeder again, and the land was a-quiver with the stirring of a trillion tulip bulbs. All very nice, all very sunny.

And Opening Day was just around the corner.

Which meant that, along with keen anticipation rising like maple sap, I was feeling, simultaneously, a sticky woe descend.

Let me introduce, at this point, Stan, the good neighbor. He's more than that. He's a prince. I like Stan a lot, enjoy his company when we're on the morning train, relish our conversation. But that conversation invariably leads past kids and school and even rock 'n' roll to, of course, baseball. And Stan's a Yankee fan. And he knows what I am. Stan is ever polite about mortal affairs. "D'ya think the Sox helped themselves this winter?" he asked me in that early spring of '03, as if the question were not rhetorical, as if the Yanks had not, that particular Hot Stove, signed Contreras from directly beneath our collective Sox schnozz, meanwhile fouling the Colon deal via Chicago. "I don't know if they helped themselves," Stan will aver, nice as can be. Stan will, at conversation's end, quietly tell me how he recently upped his dish-TV subscription so that he can get all the games, from everywhere in the universe, including semipro contests from Havana and Osaka. He says it quietly because he's a nice guy, and what he's offering is, finally, "If you ever want to watch a Sox game after the kids are asleep, c'mon over." I like Stan a lot, but . . .

It's impossible.

Stan does not know, but would not be surprised to learn, that I am a BLOHARD. Have been since '85, when I first met and wrote about the then all-but-anonymous Benevolent Loyal Order of Honorable and Ancient Red Sox Diehard Sufferers of New York. Among us Sox fans— among you, if you're with us now that we're World Champs—the BLOHARDS are, today, something bordering on semi-famous. ESPN found out about us in early '04, and FOX followed, as FOX is wont to do. We got better known throughout the season, and Jim Shea now tells me the membership roll is climbing up to some crazy number like two thousand. Backpackers are certainly among our rookies, certinally, but, hey, what the hell. They're paying their dues.

It wasn't this way with the BLOHARDS when I joined in '85, and it surely wasn't anything like this way back in the early '60s, when a championship of any kind appeared impossibly far off to even the truest of believers.

Men such as Jim Powers.

He was, forty-plus years ago, a man in exile—a man like I am today, a man like he still is, a man precisely like the one Aeschylus conjured when he wrote in *Agamemnon,* "I know how men in exile feed on dreams of hope." Powers was living in Connecticut and working in New York, but it was all Siberia to him. To hazard an even more purple metaphor, his world had become a large cell. The bars were pinstripes. There were pinstripes on his commuter train, pinstripes on his subway, and pinstripes in his office, all reminding him of those damned pinstriped Yankees winning pennant after pennant up in the Bronx. Powers hated pinstripes and he hated the Yankees. In the early '60s, the Yanks were the last team standing almost every year, so New York was a tough town for a Sox fan to be in—as it would be, and for all the same reasons, for us in the '90s.

Because of his persuasion, Powers, who had been born in Uxbridge, thirty-six miles from Fenway, was shunned and ridiculed by his colleagues. As Aeschylus knew, exile doesn't dampen the inner flames, it fans them. Powers walked about Manhattan subsisting on his unreasonable dreams of hope, becoming leaner but prouder and more defiant. Such people are dangerous, and by 1965 Powers was poised to commit a desperate act.

He was sitting in the bar of J.J.'s Cellar, a restaurant on East Fifty-fifth Street, hidden in a sea of pinstriped suits at cocktail hour. Significantly, Powers was not alone. He was huddling with others who shared his misery and his sense of mission. The names they whispered were foreign to midtown Manhattan. Not Ruth, Gehrig, Mantle, and Joe but Ruth (as a pitcher), Foxx, Williams, and Dom. The group recounted bygone Boston glories and dared to predict future victories. From such hushed intercourse, movements are born. These renegades with their neckties, bow ties, wingtips, and dedication to the Sox weren't unlike Hancock, Revere, and the gang, huddling in that tavern in Lexington and banging down whatever it was that Sam Adams was brewing back in April of 1775.

"We'd get twelve, fourteen guys together and have a couple of cocktails," Powers told me in 1985 when first I asked him about the BLOHARDS. He was treating me to a nice lunch at the Yale Club, so the place where it all came 'round for me and Jane in the aftermath of the glorious championship is the place where it all began. "We were basically transplanted New Englanders. We didn't call ourselves the BLOHARDS then. That came a couple of years later, when I was thinking about that benevolent-loyal-order stuff of the Grangers back in Uxbridge."

Although it took some time and rumination to come up with the official acronym, these guys were always BLOHARDS—that's what brought them together. Like Powers, who spent much of his career as ad director of *Family Weekly* and then *USA Weekend,* many of the founding fathers were in the media business. By nature, they were blowhards.

The BLOHARDS gained in organization and sophistication, the membership growing to 150, 250, 350 and more. Officers were selected by Powers, and he became president. "He is the always and forever leader," was how one member put it to me, back when. "The BLOHARDS without Jim would be the Vatican without the Pope."

The BLOHARDS convened, perforce, beyond the DMZ: in the New England Room of the Hotel Lexington, in the fiftieth floor dining room of the McGraw-Hill Building, *even in the Combo Room of Yankee Stadium.* Can you imagine 138 BLOHARDS no more than a short fly ball from Steinbrenner's box? It happened in the '70s.

Over the seasons the BLOHARDS grew stronger, and their ever more reckless bravado proved irresistible to recruits. A lonely Henry Berry, who was also at the Yale Club lunch with myself and Powers, had been riding a late train to his home in Darien, Connecticut, one night many years ago. He had just been to the Stadium, where the Red Sox had lost, naturally, to the Yankees. "I was deep in my thoughts of despair," Berry remembered, "when all of a sudden, from the back of the car, I heard four or five voices raised in song." It was the refrain of a folk song indigenous to New England: "Better than his brother Joe, Dominic Di-Mag-giooooooo!" Curious and emboldened, Berry made his way through the car and found Powers leading the chorus. "He seemed to resemble the immortal 'Nuf Sed McGreevey, a leader of the Royal Rooters of the early 1900s. I introduced myself by offering a toast to the great Jimmie Foxx. By mentioning Ol' Double X, I promptly identified myself as a Red Sox fan."

Powers recognized a staunch and courageous leader when he saw one, and it was not long before Berry was a lieutenant on the rise within the BLOHARDS brigade. He narrated the slide shows at BLOHARDS gatherings and introduced honored guests, who came to bolster the troops. Johnny Pesky met with the BLOHARDS twice, and DiMaggio, Dom, addressed a gathering at the New England Room. Cleveland Amory and Peter Golenbock debated the relative merits of the Sox and Yanks at a BLOHARDS-sponsored forum. Managers talked strategy.

"Billy Herman was the best of them," remembered Berry, "but Zim is not gonna win any after-dinner awards."

As the comment indicates, Berry was wont to zing. His slide shows were raucous, ribald, sometimes even risqué, and seldom were they kindhearted. If they were hilarious to some, they weren't to all. Young Roger Clemens, a rook, seemed bewildered by the BLOHARDS when he was a guest at the first club lunch I attended. And, memorably, Butch Hobson, when he was manager, threatened to take us on en masse during his remarks after Berry had tweaked Hobson's third-base coach, the immortal Zimmer, in commentary during the slide show. Hobson really was fuming. It was a tense moment. I don't think it had anything to do with Butch's cocaine problem, but I could be wrong.

I should say, many of us BLOHARDS, myself included, have a soft spot for Zimmer. Just last year, when I and a tablemate were dissecting Francona during a lunch in the Time-Life Building, I wondered aloud how many World Series Zim might've led the Sox to in a wild-card era. "Yeah," said the other fellow. "Zim wasn't so bad." The Sox were going pretty well at that time in the spring of '04, and in such periods, when the boys are winning at a reasonable clip, the BLOHARDS are sweet and charitable folk.

Berry's banter at club dinners, and his dedication, loyalty, and inestimable bravery—he did not leave the hall when Hobson shifted to full throttle, and threatened to fully throttle the next BLOHARD to speak—eventually earned Henry the senior vice presidency of the club. Powers, Berry, and Walter Teitz became (and for many years remained) the heart of the BLOHARDS lineup. Powers ruled, Berry regaled, and Teitz collected the dues, much of which was channeled to various anti-Yankee activities—the lunches, the formal debates, especially the ceremonial case of Narragansett Beer, the essential ingredient of the quintessential BLOHARDS function: the Opening Day Bus Trip.

I am sad to report that, of the triumvirate, only Powers lived to lay hands upon the world championship trophy. Life is not fair.

As to the bus trip: When I met the BLOHARDS in '85, this was already a sixteen-year tradition. In it, the exiled traveled back, literally and figuratively, to the homeland. I joined them in the bus that year, and observed that they seemed to become younger by the mile as the bus rolled north through New England. It was something confirmed a time or two more, back in the '80s—back when I was a better BLOHARD.

I don't know where the bus leaves from these days—it's hardly a fitting outing for Caroline or Jack or Mary Grace (who wouldn't be allowed anyway), so I no longer go. But back then, when Berry was in charge of it, the tradition was for the bus to pull away from a specific curb in Westport, Connecticut. "The trip starts in front of Mario's bar," Powers told me emphatically, when giving me my first marching orders. This only substantiated for me an already pretty solid conviction that such establishments played a large part in BLOHARDS lore. If this club left plaques to mark its memories, many would be affixed to various watering holes throughout the Northeast. When confronted with that theory, Powers demurred. "We're a nice, quiet, refined group," he insisted. "For instance, on the bus trip, there is a rule: No drinking until the bus passes Bridgeport"—which is nine miles from Westport—"unless absolutely necessary."

Powers was in good spirits that morning back in '85, resplendent in his bright Red Sox sweater and a pair of nearly as bright lime green slacks. Although he was already a man of more than fifty years, that day he was a teenager. He stood at the head of the bus and addressed forty BLO-HARDS squirming in their seats. He laid out the Bridgeport rule. The bus was a sea of Red Sox caps and painter's hats (remember the trend?) embossed with nick-names of the era—DEWEY, BIG FOOT, HIT MAN (remember them?). On some of the older hats: YAZ.

We were off. Very quickly, Westport was in the rear-view mirror, and Berry announced that the bar was official-ly open. The BLOHARDS broke out the beer and cigars.

The pilgrimage followed the forever route, due east, then north for Hartford. They cheered Berry in Bridgeport, and they cheered him anew in Hartford. Berry had been born in Hartford, a place that, entirely due to Berry, had assumed a hallowed significance in BLOHARDS lore. Berry, who as a Connecticut lad could have gone either way (Sox or Yanks), had, as he says, "grown up under the spell of Sox radio announcer Fred Hoey." Berry's grandfather, Bunts Berry, was the first man in the history of Hartford to bunt, having laid one down in 1878. "The Ballad of Bunts Berry" used to be dutifully recited each April as the bus passed the old East Hartford cutoff. The year I traveled with the BLO-HARDS, Berry himself delivered the rendition of the legendary tale. Maybe Powers still tells of Bunts Berry during the bus trip, maybe another old-timer like Dick Durrell has taken up the task. I don't know. The nouveau BLOHARDS seem more taken with "Tessie," a lyric the Royal Rooters used to sing to rouse the crowd back at the turn of the last century. Sox management unearthed the tune, and the story behind it, a year or two ago, and Dr. Charles—that's Charles Steinberg, the magician of community relations for the Henry/Lucchino gang—arranged for the Boston band Dropkick Murphys to make a new recording. It's pretty good, but . . . I just don't know. "Tessie" belongs to everyone in the Nation, anyone with the ninety-nine cents to download it. "Bunts Berry" belonged to the BLOHARDS. I hope someone in the membership still remembers how it goes.

As Berry sat down after his stirring tribute to his grandfather, copies of the *1985 BLOHARDS Quiz* were handed out. It was a simple test for any fanatical fan, and the bus trippers were, to a man, fanatical fans.

- Which of the following never hit a home run in a crucial Yankee-Red Sox game? A) Bucky Dent, B) Johnny Lindell, C) Roy White, D) Jim Rice.
- The last bunt at Fenway Park: A) rolled foul, B) was

not scored as a sacrifice, C) occurred during the
father-son game, D) was called a "waste of time,"
by Don Zimmer.

- The Fenway "bleacher bums" are: A) now attending
Boston College hockey games, B) credited with
inventing the "wine cooler," C) opposed to baseball's
drug rules, D) seldom invited to Mark Clear's
house.

- The American League hitter most feared by the
Red Sox is: A) Eddie Murray, B) Dave Winfield,
C) Kirk Gibson, D) Glenn Hoffman.

To the BLOHARDS, that last one was a howler. They
couldn't contain themselves. "Hoffman! Haw, *Haw!!*
Sheesh. Hoffman!!"

The reminiscing began. "Yeah," claimed one BLO-
HARD, "I was at the '78 playoff game," (That gave him
points, even though the game featured every BLOHARD's
darkest nightmare). "I went to that entire last series against
Toronto" (more points). "No," said another, "I honestly was
not at Game Six of the '75 Series" (deduction), "but I went
to an earlier Series game" (add a few). "Frank Malzone? Bill
Monbouquette? Eddie Bressoud? Sure—saw 'em all as a
kid."

It was me making that last comment. I was loosening
up. "Remember this?" I asked, and began in my cracked,

altogether awful tenor. "Hi, neighbor, have a 'Gansett/Give that lager beer a chance it/Has that straight from the barrel taste . . ." A couple of others joined in: "In bottle, can, on tap it's great/Yes 'Gansett's got the flavor/Nar-ra-gan-sett flavor/A taste that's light/But not too light/Straight from the barrel taste/That's right!/That's 'Gansett."

"God," said one BLOHARD, "It seemed like Curt Gowdy played that every inning. It seemed like it was the only commercial he had."

As for our getting it right, a BLOHARD elder chipped in: "Too easy." He was right.

"Our membership seems to get younger and younger," Berry said, back then, even before the '86 team had reenergized the Nation big time. "Very few are left who remember Black Jack Wilson and Fritz Ostermueller from the '30s. Whatever . . . The club is prospering. There has been serious talk of starting a BLOHARDS chapter in Chicago— there are plenty of Red Sox fans there. Most of them don't recall Irene Hennessey, but they root for the Sox. That's what counts."

"Who was Irene Hennessey?" I asked.

Berry looked at me. "Why," he answered finally, "She's the one who sang the 'Have a 'Gansett' jingle." He paused. "I assumed you knew." It's not always easy, being a BLO-HARD.

But Berry was right when he declared that, among the BLOHARDS, all that matters is loving the Sox. Breeding, position, intelligence, wealth—these things don't mean much when you're wearing a baseball cap. This salient fact was acted out, in a way, as the bus parked behind Fenway, and the unsteady BLOHARDS piled out and headed gleefully for the window to pick up tickets that had been left for them by Arthur Moscato, the estimable ticket director, and Dick Bresciani, the cherished media-relations chief. There were, presumably, some pretty bright and pretty successful people in this ragtag, slightly sodden assemblage. But all they were at the moment was Red Sox fans, and—excepting a Little League single by a son or daughter, or the birth of a grandchild—this was about as happy as they could be in this life.

There were more BLOHARDS inside Fenway. Suzyn Waldman, down on the field singing the national anthem, was introduced to the crowd as being from New York (boos) and Boston (cheers). Yes, sports fans, *that* Suzyn Waldman—the one who has been, in recent years, in the employ of George Steinbrenner and his YES Network, the one slated to step in for Charlie Steiner in the radio booth when Charlie heads for Los Angeles to be Vin Scully's sidekick in the '05 season. Here's something to suck on, Yankee fans: In the 1980s and '90s Waldman was a BLO-

HARD, her dues were always paid up. Her dog in 1985 was named Fenway. I'm betting that if she still has a dog, he's named Fenway Two or Fenway Three. We're everywhere. And Suzyn, you're outed.

BLOHARDS all over the lot. There was a big BLO-HARD in Section 22, Row 21, Seat 14 (name withheld). He was a school administrator from Manhattan who sheepishly admitted to me that he was "playing hooky." He had called too late to get a seat on the bus, but had driven up nonetheless.

There was a BLOHARD sitting next to him (name withheld) who was in private debate over the wisdom of ordering a beer "even in this frigid weather." He ordered two.

There was a BLOHARD in Row 19 (name not even sought). He was in the end seat next to a pretty young Bostonian. He could have been her father, but that wasn't what he was trying to be.

The BLOHARDS had an active and exciting day at Fenway, and so did the Red Sox. The Hose, who were showing signs of life in the mid-1980s—showing signs of being the team they would be right through the '90s—eventually hosed the Yanks 9-2, and the game immediately became part of BLOHARDS lore. Attendance at this opener became something that would earn you points at future club functions.

Happily, very happily, the BLOHARDS headed back to their bus. They settled into their seats, cracked open 'Gansetts and started chattering away in BLOHARDS fashion. "Surely Oil Can Boyd will win 20 games this season, and surely the Sox will score 900 runs . . . Surely we'll finish ahead of the Yanks, surely we'll win the pennant . . . Surely we'll be World Champions, just like we were only yesterday, in 1918 . . ." One by one, BLOHARDS fells asleep. When they awoke, they were back in New York, exiles again, forced anew to take what nourishment they might from those unreasonable dreams of hope.

No dreams came true in 1985, certainly, and if a few of them did during the thrilling 1986 campaign, that long ordeal finally came to a denouement as painful—and destined to be as immortal—as 1978's. I went to all seven games of the '86 World Series, and was so wasted at its bitter end, I promised myself I'd never do such a thing again.

Well, you never know. And you shouldn't make promises you're not likely to keep.

The BLOHARDS persevered, of course, even prospered, through all the disappointments that preceded '04. That was their mission since Powers founded the club, it seemed—to persevere. As for me, my life went through changes. Luci and I married in 1995 and started having kids, then we moved from the city out to Westchester.

As I say, I don't go on the bus trips anymore, but I still

go to the spring and autumn lunches, which have moved around town from corporate cafeterias in midtown to the National Guard Armory on the Upper East Side to, now, the Yale Club, near Grand Central. We land where Powers can find us seats and an open bar.

Where I live these days, I cannot share the BLO-HARDS. I've thought of inviting Stan, the good neighbor, to a BLOHARDS lunch as my guest. Ultimately, I always decide against it. Yes, he might get a kick out of it at first, but eventually all the Yankee bashing would get to him. It's the reason I don't stroll across the street to watch the Sox on his super-dish, but settle for the radio feed on the Internet. My rationalization is that baseball's a radio game anyway, but the fact is Stan and I—who are essentially the same guy, from opposite sides of the aisle—are too prickly about certain things to be sitting side-by-side when Jeter jacks one. Or Ortiz does.

It's not just Stan. It's Dan over the eastern stone wall, and Steve over the northern one. It's Brendan next door. It's Eric, directly across from Stan. It's Jon, directly across from us. Stan and Eric grew up in Brooklyn, Dan and Steve in Queens, and Jon in the Bronx. I think Brendan is from around here—this town, or another Westchester town. I think he's from Armonk, one village over. They're New Yorkers, Yanks fans one and all. What none of them is, not in the remotest, is a New Englander.

Luci and I have lost our accents—something that we're reminded of, whenever we go north—but we remain intrinsically, instinctively unlike our neighbors in several unseen and unheard ways. I'm not talking about B-hats and such, I'm talking about subtleties, and things that happen behind closed doors—all of it informing who we are, and all of it somehow pertinent to this Red Sox question.

Luci was born in Pennsylvania and didn't get to Chelmsford until junior high, therefore is less of a New Englander than I am. Her crew socks, for example, do not have holes in them. She uses them for rags if they get even one or two little holes, which is an astonishingly spendthrift philosophy, it seems to me. She is even more firmly dedicated to keeping the kids' wardrobes pristine. If Jack gets a stain that cannot be removed, into the Salvation Army box goes the shirt. Only Caroline's very best hand-me-downs are designated for Mary Grace. Others get the items that are deemed not-Mary Grace-worthy. "I want the children to look nice," Luci explains simply—but I suspect something.

"You're not trying to turn them against me?" I have asked her on more than one occasion.

I've asked the question because, as regards clothes, if Luci has been what society might see as on the mend ever since leaving New England and arriving in Manhattan, I have been just as strenuously recalcitrant. No, I no longer own the plaid watch cap, but I do still have a lot of plaid, and I harbor some truly dorkish but warm wool hats. Many of my sweaters are more lumpish than stylish, and I would suppose I own as much chamois—*shammy*—as anyone in a hundred-mile radius. "L.L. Bean" is too *luxe* a term to describe my weekend wear. I have more than one pair of cotton sweats, and I go out jogging in public wearing them, with one of those wool hats pulled low over my ears.

I do own a few suits, but hasten to add that they, and most of my shirts and neckties, came from Filene's Basement—the Boston flagship store. (You can get a Southwick's there for little more than a C-note, if you stalk it right.) I own more than a couple pair of boots, from hiking to cowboy, and as we'll see shortly, the latter came in mighty handy during the Cowboy Up! campaign. And I have five pair of chinos, including two from Beans that are shammy lined. So, now that I think about it, there are things about us that are not necessarily unseen and unheard, and that might tip the observant bystander to an underlying New Englandness.

But the bystander doesn't get to see me eat, which I energetically do, New England-style, in the privacy of our kitchen. Were he to see me eat, he would know his mark for sure. I enjoy—I don't mean ingest, I mean really enjoy—creamy clam chowder, fried clams, lobster rolls with mayo, anything with tartar sauce, brown bread with raisins, baked beans, cod, Indian Pudding with maple syrup, bread pudding with maple syrup, oatmeal with maple syrup, an oatmeal crème brulee thing that Luci cooks up, French toast with maple syrup, anything with apples in the autumn, squash pie (more than pumpkin, and, hey, use a little maple syrup in the recipe), vanilla ice cream, vanilla pudding, vanilla extract, vanilla ice cream with maple syrup, vanilla pudding with maple syrup, finnan haddie (like they serve it at Locke-Ober's), and a cold-as-ice martini (like they serve it at the Ritz, and I don't mean the one on Central Park, I mean the one overlooking the Public Gardens). A place not far from us called Crabtree's Kittle House—it's in a village called Chappaqua, famous now as the place where Hill and Bill live—knows whereof I speak. But even it doesn't go far enough. I am the South Beach antichrist.

My Yankee-rooting neighbors notwithstanding, almost immediately after our family moved to Westchester from the city, I found the county enabling. I was suddenly surrounded not only by establishments like Crabtree's and others of near-equal rustic charm, but by private farms and public (we're always taking Jack and Mary Grace to see the animals over at Muscoot Farm, which is one of my favorite haunts, too), and by stone walls, hills, trees, and back roads that were just as inscrutable as those that I remembered from my youth. I could sometimes imagine I was back home, if I drew a deep breath, shut my eyes and, particularly, my ears.

However, if I didn't turn off the audio, someone was bound to proclaim a mere hillock "quite a mountain" or a reservoir "a lake." Things like that get in amongst us New Englanders, just like the BLOHARDS would get in amongst Stan. New Englanders know a mountain when we see one, and are certain Winnipesauke or the Rangeleys are more naturally splendid than any dammed thing.

During the winter of '03, which immediately preceded that free-flowing spring—a winter whose harshness I've already referenced—I had a brief illusion. After the biggest of the many big snowfalls, I drove the family to a terrific dude ranch for kids, Rocking Horse Ranch, just outside New Paltz, which is another New York hamlet posing as a New England hamlet. On Day One, I might have been in New Hampshire. There were horses and horse smells. We got Caroline, who was by then five, on skis for the first time, and she rode a rope tow that reminded her dad of the one he had cut his teeth (and mittens) on when he was a lad. (Mine was in Groton, Massachusetts, on the swales of what was, in summer, the public Groton C.C. golf course; I add things to this Bosox meditation as I remember them, and I hope that's okay with you.) Caroline skated on a frozen pond with Mom, as Dad and the twins, who were two-and-a-half, built a snowman family, a replica of ourselves. We took a horse-drawn wagon ride through the winter woods, and Jack and I harmonized on "Jingle Bells," even though it was weeks after the Yule. Jack proclaimed the ride "fun," and Mary Grace said the same about her go-round on Red, the thirty-eight-year-old horse who had been put out to pasture to service the tots. For all I knew, I was walking through a land sketched by Currier and Ives.

But the next morning at breakfast, I started to notice things. Bagels instead of doughnuts at the buffet. Maple syrup that I'm pretty sure wasn't from Vermont. Things started creeping in.

By Day Three, something that had gone completely unseen during my earlier reverie was, suddenly and ferociously, apparent. Every fourth—every third!—person was wearing a Yankees cap—here a ball cap, there a wool cap, all with the Evil Empire insignia. As kids got out of the indoor pool, every fifth one pulled on a Yankees T-shirt. Every tenth one was a Mets fan, or the offspring of a Mets fan who had bought Mets garb at Christmastime. I was in Dante's cistern, swimming against an irreversible tide of terror, getting sucked down, dizzily, toward the drain.

It fairly, finally dawned on me. I'm not in New England anymore.

That night I had a conversation with Luci.

"Honey," I said. "We live in Westchester."

"Very good."

"Now then, how do we raise New Englanders?"

"What do you mean?"

"How do we bring up the kids to be New Englanders?"

"Well, we can't, can we?"

"We have to raise New Yorkers?"

"Technically, yes."

I thought this over. "Well, I'm going to fight it. Starting here, starting now. April's just around the corner."

So I called Mom in Massachusetts and asked her to go over to Marshall's and buy up all the Bosox garb she could find for kids ages two, two, and five. Days later, her CARE package arrived containing little hats in blue and pink, each bearing the stylized "B," little red socks—sorry, I mean sox—a bunch of t-shirts, some Red Sox underpants for Jack. I sorted the clothing into three piles, put these in a corner of our bedroom, and waited for Opening Day.

And then it came, and the boys of summer went back to work, down in the Bronx and up at Fenway. And with that began a nineteen-month ride that none of us—not me, not you, not even them—will ever forget. My kids had the proper uniforms now, but who could possibly have predicted what they were in for?

The ethereal light of 2004 does not seem quite so heavenly unless seen in relief of the gloom of 2003. And so, before the dawn, the darkness.

THE REGULAR SEASON of 2003 I spent weeding, painting the patio, typing in my office, pushing the kids on the swings, walking or jogging the dog, talking on the front porch with Luci in the evenings, ultimately raking the fallen leaves—all of it with Joe Castiglione and Jerry Trupiano providing the dulcet soundtrack, either streaming through my computer speakers if I was indoors, or crackling out of the boom box if I was out, having floated down on the breezes from that station in Hartford, the same one that Henry Berry had listened to as a boy, the westernmost outpost of the Red Sox Radio Network—the one that reaches out, if fraily, to the exiles. The notion came to me early and stayed with me through the season that the 2003 Bosox were a good team—a mighty team—and when the playoff tournament took shape I said to Luci, "They actually might do something in the next few weeks." A prudent guy most of the time, that was as far as I would go—and even as I said it, I sensed I had gone too far.

Very shortly after the playoffs started, that rash declaration could have been taken as a madman's ravings—or those of a Red Sox fan—as Oakland strutted confidently toward their berth in the American League Championship Series, where surely the Yankees would greet them.

But then the Sox won a game. Anything might happen in a short series, right? They won another, and we were delivered at Game Five. Hmmmm. I started to think we might get through, the fact that the game was being played out there on the Left Coast notwithstanding.

Others were feeling that way, too. On the morning of the Saturday when that crazy, fantastic imbroglio with the A's was scheduled to end, the whole family went to Caroline's soccer game in our B-hats, to the mall in our B-hats, and lastly to Stevenson's Orchard in our B-hats. At this last stop we picked out our Halloween pumpkins, had some warm cider, and bought some pies. It was all very bucolic, all very autumnal. As we headed for the car so that Daddy might get home in time to see if we could possibly solve Tim Hudson, a kid wearing a BOSTON SUCKS T-shirt approached and, for my edification and that of my wife and our sweet children, reiterated verbally the sentiment of his shirt, adding, "And we're gonna kick your ass." We hadn't even got past Oakland yet, and at that point it time it didn't seem as if we necessarily would, but this young excrescence already had the match-up inked.

In October, of '04, advocates on both sides were wary of a second summit meeting in the ALCS, because they had seen how the previous year's bloodbath had softened the Yankees for the Marlins. But in '03, everyone in the Northeast was a-drool. No one wanted the Twins, no one wanted the A's. Yanks fans were cheering for us and we were cheering for the Yanks. Everyone in both camps wanted that series, that year, with that cast of characters. The Bosox had broken the all-time slugging percentage record of the 1927 Yankees that year, and old Fatass Clemens, in his "last year of baseball"—*Ha!*—was still throwing smoke. The Sox' new owners had come right out and called the Yankees the Evil Empire, and King George, who may or may not know "unhinged" when he sees it, speculated that these gentlemen now in charge of the Boston franchise might be unhinged. The Yanks and Sox had already battled, sometimes epically, nineteen times that year. The Yanks had won ten, the Sox nine, and the Sox had dominated all statistical categories.

This would be good, if . . .

Then Tejada screwed up. Derek Lowe did his obscene fist pump on the Oakland mound (our tormented Derek, built for endgame *dramitas,* then and to come) and we were headed back to New York. It was time to get it on.

Would I be going to the games?

Silly question. I had had seventeen years to heal.

I have hardly any talents at all that place me beyond the ordinary, but I possess a relatively keen—an *uncanny*—ability to have tickets to big-time postseason athletic events attach themselves to me for face value whenever I want them to. They are not always good seats, but they are, as we say, "in the ballpark." This was the case when I attended those seven games in '86, and it was the case in the fall of '03 when I suddenly found myself in possession of two for Game One, four for Two, four for Four, two each for Five, Six, and Seven. That left me wanting only for Game Three, the monumentally hyped shootout in Fenway involving Pedro and the Rocket. For that one, which had a scalp on its head worth $3,000 (and we're talking bleachers), I would get credentialed (i.e., gratis tickets)—another little trick of the trade I have acquired in my maturity.

Although I did want—need—to be at that game, I hasten to add: I didn't want to get credentialed, money saved notwithstanding. A credential comes with two responsibilities, neither of which I particularly welcome. The first is that one must, to express it bluntly, put a lid on it. There is No Cheering In The Press Box, and this is usually fine by me, but not when it comes to Sox-Yanks.

Also, a credential usually means you're working. So, burdened by guilt, I approached Mark at Time.com and said, "Hey, you want a blog of sorts from the ALCS? I was hoping to see it all from the stands, and I was going to ask if you wanted a fan's eye view, but now I really have to ask because, well, I'm credentialed for Game Three—and I've got this massive Irish Catholic conscience working on me and . . ." Mark put up his hand as if to say, "Enough," and said instead, "Sure." As a webmeister, he was always looking for "content," and at that moment in time I looked to him like 6'3", 195 pounds of content.

So I was going to watch these games, and I was going to write. But what was I going to write about? Sox-versus-Yanks, to be sure. But what did that mean to me? To others? What was Sox-versus-Yanks these days, and why had it come to matter *so very much to so very many?*

I'll tell you honestly, I used to root for the Mick. I was a kid. I'd cheer for Mickey to crank one in the top of the inning, then for Yaz to answer in the bottom. Dad would ask me why I was hoping the enemy would get ahead and I would answer, "He's Mickey Mantle." My dad would ask a second question, and a third: "But don't you want the Red Sox to win? Don't you hate the Yankees?" "Sure," I would answer, but even as a child I realized that was just for my father's edification. I *suppose* I hated the Yankees, but . . . well, it was nothing like I would come to hate them. It was fun then. And mild. It was childlike and sweet and, frankly, it was baseball. It wasn't mortal, and it wasn't war.

It was interesting to many of us longtime Sox fans, when we were standing in 2003 at the start line of the epochal nineteen months, just how feverish and large and, particularly, *angry* Red Sox Nation had become. I employed some excruciatingly strained hyperbole (not to mention overripe metaphor) only shortly ago in describing Jim Powers' life behind bars in the '60s, all of that silly "pinstripe" riffing. But, really, while it was fun to riff—'t'wasn't really true. Powers will tell you as quickly as anyone, it was all a game back then. He was a happy-go-lucky guy, amused by his little fraternity of fellow sufferers. These days, apparently, it was no longer play acting. We listened to boiling mad sports-talk radio; we turned over cars in Kenmore Square; we set bonfires on the University of New Hampshire campus an hour north of Boston—and we did this when we beat a who-cares California team in the American League Division Series. Not the Championship Series, the *Division* Series.

We accounted for sixty-plus regular season sellouts at the Fens one season, then followed that with eighty-one the next. We did all sorts of mad things, and if we were like this a century ago in 1903, when our Boston Americans won the first-ever World Series (and, by the way, we were *just* like this back then, from what I've read), then we were not like this when Jim Powers turned into a Red Sox fan, or when I did.

I'll give you the briefest evidence, and you won't believe it's true, but it is. In 1978 the Red Sox frittered away that all-but-mathematically-insurmountable loss-column lead over the Yankees in the waning weeks of summer. I was living in New Hampshire at the time, and I remember calling Jake in Massachusetts as the Sox were about to play their last game of the season.

"Bag," I said. "Am I wrong, or are the Sox but one game out?"

"They are one out," Jake confirmed.

"Am I wrong that if Tiant wins today at Fenway and the Yanks lose in the Stadium, there will be a playoff tomorrow?"

"You are right, sir!" Bag answered. He had a trademark Ed McMahon thing that was amusing to his closest friends and to precious few others. His sister thought him a fool. Annie would, too, once she married him.

And so the Bag and I drove into town, walked up and bought grandstand seats. Yes we did; no problem. The fans had become so disgusted with the team after suffering through the Yankees' Boston Massacre four-game set in August, they weren't half-filling the park for what might turn out to be a tie-making win. As for the Bag and me, we watched from very good grandstand seats as the only score they posted on the Green Monster that day indicated that Rick Wise and the Cleveland Indians were getting the better of the Yanks in New York, while El Tiante was laboring mightily to prevail in the contest at hand. Once it was clear that the Sox would triumph and that the playoff, for which we had already won a flip of the coin, would be played in Boston the next day, it was announced that available tickets for that game would go on sale at the ticket booths right after the final out. Bag and I sauntered to the gated window, easily beating the Johnny Come Latelies—the backpack-ers—who were now bombing in on the Mass Pike from Newton and Wellesley. We scooped up a fistful of bleacher seats for the Monday game. Then we repaired to the Dugout bar on Comm Ave and decided which associates we would call on the pay phone and invite to the historic contest. Our many dear friends and kinfolk thereby got the privilege of witnessing . . .

Bucky Dent. But that's not the point.

The point is that, yes, there has long been a Sox-Yanks rivalry, but it has had its ups and downs, its ebbs and flows of passion. The point is the 162nd game of the storied 1978 season was not near a sellout, and you can look it up. I seri-ously doubt there was much of a rivalry between Boston and New York in the '20s and '30s because the Sox were so poor, and I know the same was generally true from '60 through '66. In the years since, the fight has been joined on occasion—'78, '99, a few races for the division title—but I've never seen it like it is in the new millennium. If it is true (and I'm sure it is) that, in the free-agent universe we live in, most of the players on either side do not hate their opposite number as Munson hated Fisk, it is nonetheless evident that the fans have taken this thing past wit's end in recent years. "I remember one of my first opening games against the Red Sox, with the Rocket pitching, looking out at him," Bernie Williams reminisced just before the start of the 2003 ALCS. "That was my first glimpse of how intense it was. Fans from each side just wanting to beat each other up. I remember looking into the stands and seeing people fighting. It was loud and packed and a rude awakening. To me it was, 'Welcome to Yankees–Red Sox.'"

And now, October of 2003, welcome to Yankees–Red Sox. Here we go.

LUCI HAD SUGGESTED I might ask my buddy Mike Padden to accompany me to Game One, but I couldn't do it. Mike, one of my dearest friends, is what I consider the world's worst kind of fan. He grew up in Manchester, New Hampshire, and attended the same New England college that I did. He landed in New York City about the same time I did, having taken a job with the public defenders office out in Brooklyn. It was, maybe, '84 or '85 when I bumped into Mike while jogging in Central Park. We did some catching up over the course of two or three miles. I learned on that summer's day that Mike had come to love all things New York—I was very happy for him—then I learned that this extended even to his having become, good God, a Yankees fan. I was appalled at the time; I remain appalled. Mike and I can attend and have attended and will attend Sox–Yanks games, because he is a sweet soul—it's never going to be an itchy situation, as with me and Stan—

but for Game One, I needed a fellow traveler by my side, and so this would be Jane, originally from Wellesley. It would have been Luci, of course, but when it comes to mid-week Yankee Stadium games, even post-season, she needs for it to be a seventh-game kind of thing.

After work, Jane and I took the D train north to the Bronx and as we emerged from the subway station, the sky above us exploded with unearthly thunder. That's a mighty phrase, but, really, we almost dove to the sidewalk, our post-9/11 instincts kicking in. What had happened was, the F-14 fighter planes that would, in one half-second, fly low over the stadium as part of the Game One opening cere-monies had just *whooshed* directly over our heads. Now we were good and jittery and ready for some baseball.

The seats I had been able to secure for the Yankee Stadium games really did, as a Yankee fan might put it, suck. We were in the bleachers, Sec. 57, Row N, Seats 18 and 19. Realizing this ahead of time, we made a prudent decision to wear no Bosox garb, for we knew the bleachers in both Yankee Stadium and Fenway were vigorously, dan-gerously (if seldom mortally) hostile to members of the other tribe.

To my surprise, the bleacher gang in the stadium was a bit more civil than I remembered it from earlier years, and I think there were three reasons for this. First, the bleach-ers had become the No Alcohol Bleachers, and that meant you couldn't so much as buy a 3.2 beer beneath the stands. Second, it was the nature of the post-season to have people like, well, me and Jane—who could get their hands on tickets somehow, and who might in fact be supporting the enemy—in these bleacher seats, squeezing out the rabid Yankees fans who had filled them during the eighty-one regular-season games. And third, in 2003 the Yanks fans seemed to have forsaken the hoary old slogan "Boston Sucks" in favor of the more inventive and certainly more dignified "Nineteen Eighteen!" Chanted over and over again at high volume, this war whoop leant to the bleachers an air of sophistication. The bleachers are seldom subtle, but there was something subtle about "Nineteen Eighteen!"

Nevertheless, Jane and I, cowards, were traveling thoroughly incognito. Others braver than we had their B-hats on, and the most flamboyant were already engaged in taunting matches with their New York counterparts. I won't say the taunting was good-natured; it was not. In fact, I saw a weird, diabolical dynamic at work in the first two or three innings. Yankee fans would goad the Beantown loudmouths into ever more demonstrative support of the Bosox, and then something—a knocked-over Coke, a thrown peanut— would take the action to another level. One of the many layers of security would rush to the scene of the crime, and at this point the Yankee fans, who of course constituted an overwhelming majority, would point as one to the Red Sox fan and would shout something that amounted to "Instigator!" The Sox fan would be escorted from the stands, his thirty dollars forfeit. I saw this happen at least four times on that first Wednesday night, twice more on Thursday. Yes, this is as reported by a dyed-in-the-wool Boston fan, which is to say through a biased lens. But I am a journalist at heart, and I say that this is what I saw. I think it was a pre-conceived plot to rid the bleachers of all Red Sox rooters. It was Bosox cleansing.

Whether it was in fact a strategy or just a methodology that developed on the fly, it had the effect of making Jane and me all the more determined to remain under cover. Jane simply sat on her hands. Beginning in about the third inning, when it was clear that Wakefield's knuckleball was devilish tonight and the Sox might get to Mussina, I determined to have some sport with my neighbors. I started issuing proclamations that never violated my Red Sox allegiance, but that could be interpreted variously by my Yankee-fan cohorts in the (sorta) cheap seats. To whit: "*Jee-zus,* he throws the thing sixty g-d miles an hour!" A mere statement of fact, which elicited this sympathetic response from the fellow to my left: "I know it! And they're swinging like Little Leaguers at it! I could hit this guy!"

"No question!" I agreed.

Things started going very well indeed in the middle innings when Ortiz launched a shot that may land any minute now, Walker followed with a foul-pole knock and Manny urged one over the fence in right center. My three reactions, as issued to seatmates:

"*Godawlmighty*, will you look at *that!* I guess you don't want to go three balls on that guy!"

"I can't believe the ump overruled the foul call!"

"*Inches!*"

All opinions were true enough, and would have been equally on target in Fenway. Life is context.

Jane risked the occasional smile at my little game, but I could tell we were in no way suspected. In fact, we began to develop friendships with those around us, and if they wondered at us not cheering the (precious few) Yankee hits and (barely more) Yankee strikeouts of Red Sox batters, it wasn't evident. The guy in front of me, a beefy lad in a T-shirt, became something of a buddy. He knew his baseball, and we began to discuss moves and countermoves. This made things trickier for me, because I couldn't very well aver that, say, Manny was the best run producer in baseball in a situation such as the present, but rather that Manny was a tough dude to be facing in this instance. Over the innings, a real baseball bond began to develop between me and this guy, and I began to feel a little badly that our relationship was based on such a cheap sham, a sham entirely of my making. If he had known me for a Sox fan, I was sure, then he would hate me. And yet here I was, knowing who and what he was, and I liked him. Disquieting, but then . . .

The Sox were comfortably ahead, 5-0. Truth be told, I was happy to be in a beer-free environment. Frustration was thick in the air above the bleachers. The Yankee fans turned at times to the other entertainments, which as a Sox fan I couldn't abide. Yankee Stadium has cloaked itself head to toe in the ambiance of NBA basketball games: super-loud music (the usual we-will-rock-you and we-are-the-champions), excruciating video games on the message boards and hackneyed between-innings shtick. Believe it or not, the infield sweepers still must dance during their 5th-inning rounds to the Village People's "YMCA." I mean, that's just gotta go. I said to Jane, "It's as if they're still playing 'the Curly Shuffle' on the message board at Shea."

I think if you had asked me before the '03 series whether there was a rule concerning the time allowed to elapse between half innings, I would have answered, "Sure. There must be. Three minutes? Four?"

But the Yankees' behavior of '03 and '04 has convinced me otherwise (and it's convinced the Twins' skip Ron Gardenhire otherwise, too). The Yankees have blown open the seventh inning stretch from interlude to intermission. It begins with a moment of silence. Fine. Then Ronan Tynan, the big lug of an Irish tenor, delivers an accappella rendition of "God Bless America," replete with the introductory verse that no one knows, plus many dramatic pauses. "Not exactly the Kate Smith version," someone sitting near me said. Then, finally, comes "Take Me Out to the Ball Game." Then, extra-finally, comes an ear-splitting, obnoxious video of a lunatic doing that thing called "The Cotton-Eye Joe." It makes "The Curly Shuffle" look like Balanchine. Now, daughter Caroline loves to do "The Cotton-Eye Joe," and she twirls her invisible lasso prettily just before doing the clap-and-shuffle sequence. But the psychopath on the Stadium message board is one disturbing bucko.

"What's with 'The Cotton-Eye Joe?'" I asked.

"Dunno," one of my new pals answered. "They've been doin' it for a coupla years."

They have? Maybe so. And for a coupla years I've been in parts of the Stadium where beer is sold, and I've been getting a beer during the newly interminable seventh-inning stretch.

Wakefield walked the first two he faced in the seventh, and was pulled by Grady. Now I was angry. I was certain the Yankees had staged that noisome between-innings crapola to rattle our pitcher. I was seeing plots and designs everywhere.

But tonight it didn't matter. The bullpen allowed only the two walkers to score, and the final was 5-2 our side, a dramatic if not exactly thrilling statement that changed the way people were looking at the series. Jane and I savored the moment, and made our way slowly down the bleachers. We looked at the very nice monuments park—Ruth, Gehrig and company—that they have in deep center, then we each made a collection of Yankee souvenir cups that had been discarded by the despondent fans. "What are we ever going to do with these?" I asked.

"Give 'em away."

Since I had four tickets for Game Two I turned it into a college reunion by inviting Art, Dave (Swoop), and Mike—yes, Mike Padden, who would finally get to a game since I could now sit alongside a traitor and also because, well, the good guys were ahead. We four are fellows who know how to insinuate ourselves into the most crowded of saloons, and this we did at Stan's—no relation to Good Neighbor Stan, but, rather, a hallowed hall-cum-dump across the street from the bleachers entrance. I had fore-warned my friends that we would be spending the game in a beer-free biosphere, and so we forsook the player intros in favor of six-bucks-a-pop brewskies and a bit of wives-and-kids talk.

Once back in good old Section 57, and having high-fived my bro in the row in front, who tonight was wearing a Harley T-shirt, I noticed that there were a lot of those caps they had been selling at Stan's on the heads of the love-ly young women here in the bleachers. They were nice blue ball caps with 1918 embroidered stylishly on the back, small, in Red Sox red with the white piping. A good dig, I thought. This 1918 and Curse of the Bambino business was coming to define this rivalry absolutely for many people.

"Haven't been to this park for years," said my friend Art, who is a big sports fan. I knew Art's team to be the Mets. I had graciously taken him to Game Seven in 1986— I'm quite a guy—but still I was surprised. "Really?" I asked.

"My kids have never seen Yankee Stadium," Art answered. "Not once." It turns out the reason is philosophical. Art would not put a dime into a baseball ticket if part of that dime might end up in George Steinbrenner's pocket. I've always considered Art to be a man of sound moral bearing, and my opinion of him only increased that night. He was quite obviously made of sterner stuff than even Yogi Berra.

Swoop is Canadian, and would just as soon have watched hockey on one of the many TVs at Stan's bar. But he seemed to be enjoying the game in the way of a man who is devoid of prejudice and malice. This I found interesting: someone appreciating a Yanks-Sox game on an aesthetic level. I wanted to get inside his head. I wanted to experience what it was like, when the Sox left all sorts of runners aboard in the first and second, to view the action as, oh, ah, a pitcher displaying guile as he emerged from a mess of his own making, rather than as an unforgivable squander. I wanted to be able to stand stock still, as Swoop did placidly as he gazed through his binoculars, rather than constantly rock back and forth, sway side to side as I had been doing for two nights now. I wanted to be Swoop, as the Sox fell further behind.

Mike and I sat side by side.

"The baby's good?"

"Fine. Jan's kinda tired, but everything's great."

"Good."

"Yeah."

"And Tommy?"

"He's fine."

"Into the Wiggles?"

"God, nothing but."

" 'Fruit salad, yummy *yummmmiieee!* ' " I sang.

"Jeez, no, not tonight!" said a blonde, obviously a young mom, in the row in front. "No Wiggles! I'm on a night off."

"Sorry," I said, understanding completely.

"How's Luci?" Mike asked. "The kids?"

"Fine. Hey, what's with your Giambi. He's kinda a big hunk of nothing."

"Oh, we love him—we love big bangers. Nice trot by Manny on the homer against the A's, by the way."

"Hey, least we admit he's a slug. Right now, he's our slug. How's your mom?"

"Good. Getting older, but good. They're coming down from Manchester next week to see the grandkids."

"Great. Hey, they still Sox fans?"

"Oh yeah, sure."

I paused here, hoping he got my point.

The battles went on between Sox and Yanks fans in the bleachers again. No fisticuffs, but some pretty earnest discord. There were a few particularly loutish Boston supporters on that Thursday, a couple of whom were removed. Most of them looked like either Matt Damon or Denis Leary. They reminded me why I liked that particular Boston team, the Class of '03. I knew all about the Cowboy Up! rally cry that the Texans—Millar, Nixon—had brought to the team, but, frankly, I was more taken by Grady's comments when he talked about his "band of renegades" who cared less about Babe Ruth and more about making sure their Harleys were working well enough to get across the Tobin Bridge on their way to Fenway. Cool, I thought. We used to be, famously, country clubbers: twenty-five cabs for twenty-five players. Now we're bikers. And it was also cool that Grady had called it the Tobin instead of the Mystic River Bridge. He sounded, even with that accent, like a local guy, and he didn't pander to the hit movie. If you didn't know the Tobin, you could look it up.

But the renegades didn't do it that night, and frankly I had some quarrels with Grady over the lineup, not to mention the early-inning running. But, hey, that's baseball. I'll dance with the guy who brung me, and that guy was Grady Little. That's how I felt—at that time.

Yankee Stadium had worn me out, and I don't think I could've taken a third night in a row there. Too big, too loud, too tense not being able to shout, *"Nomaah!!"*

On the way out of our rows, the Harley-shirted guy and I slapped hands. "See you Game Six!" he said, then added with emphasis, "Less we sweep up there."

"Yeah." We.

I got home at one o'clock again, but this time didn't go for the SportsCenter repeat. When you're 450 feet away all night, and then you are giddy with victory, you like to see what the mistake had been on the pitch to Ortiz, and just how far that sucker had truly traveled. But when you're exhausted by lack of sleep and by defeat, you want to go to bed.

The weekend began, as weekends are wont to, on Friday night—even though it was a night off from baseball. Work in the city placed me on the 6:04 to Kisco, and at the train station, there was Stan. It turned out Stan and Lissette and their kids, the delightful Jason and Brianna, were over to our place for pizza. Lucille knew which train I'd be on, and Stan had volunteered to pick me up. Of course he had.

"Stan!"

"Hey."

"How ya been?"

"Great."

"Thanks for the lift.""

"Tomorrow's a must game for you guys."

I did not reply, "What do you mean?" or, "They're all important now" or, "History indicates that a team is not eliminated until a team is eliminated" or, "Sez you" or, "Right back at ya!" I said something wuss like, "Well, it sure could be useful." For Pedro would be pitching the game in question and, yes, that might be useful—to win the Pedro game.

I had been looking forward to pizza and beer, and a night off from the *sturm-und-drang*. But when the Sox and Yanks are having at it, there is no relief, especially if friends are over for pizza and beer. Stan batted lead-off: "I couldn't believe that stunt you guys pulled against Oakland, with the L-IL-LY lettering on the back of the players' jackets. So bush league. They should have fined the franchise."

"Didn't you think it was kind of funny? Funny gag, and maybe shake Lilly up a bit?"

"So bush."

"Well, it didn't work anyway. Lilly pitched fine."

"Doesn't matter."

"What about Torre. Looking for gunk under Timlin's brim, just 'cause he's pitching well. Even Harold Reynolds on ESPN said that was bush, 'specially in the post-season."

"Not in the same class. A manager does what a manager needs to do."

"Yeah, well—. . ."

The neighborhood was getting edgy. I still delighted, as I had all season, in my morning visits at the bus stop with first-grader Reed, whose Yanks jersey was being cleaned on a once-every-three-days basis. And frankly, I figured Stan was right with most of his arguments—he's a very savvy guy, as regards baseball. But this was getting to the point where being right did not matter a whit. This was getting to be about . . . again, perspective. And Stan and I did not share perspective, I realized as I watched the conversation devolve.

"Pedro, doesn't win, I figure you're done."

"Wait a second, Mussina pitches again in this series, right?"

"Yeah, so?"

"Well, correct me, but he's pretty soft, right? Fine regular season, but soft, Oriole-type guy in the post. That about right? Eighty-eight million of soft?"

So, as I say and as you see, there was a perspective gap.

My perspective was Boston, and I needed to get to Boston—fast. On Saturday morning I took the kids to Caroline's soccer game while Luci finished packing, then we pointed the mini-van north. Mary Grace got sick just west of Hartford, and I figured this was due to the sudden lurch from Yankee territory into Bosox, like what happens to those space guys in the movies when their cheeks go all jiggly as they pass through a time warp.

The incident did not delay us crucially, and we were ensconced at my sister's house in Wellesley by three in the afternoon. My friend Jane was, like me, credentialed for the third game of that series, a contest also known by the CB-radio shorthand "Pedro-Roger" (perhaps from the enemy's standpoint, "Rocket-Pedro"). Jane arrived at her parents' home ten minutes after we landed, and her father, Mr. Bachman, graciously offered to drive Jane and me to Kenmore. "Parking'll be nuts," he said, which was what much of Boston was saying about the whole day. *Parking'll be nuts, the game'll be nuts, the city'll be nuts.*

The latter was already true. As my family and I had driven east on the Mass Pike earlier, I'd seen a van painted white-and-black in imitation of a cow, with this slogan on its side, "THE BOSTON RED SOX—COWBOY UP!" In passing under an electronic message board meant to tell us of traffic tie-ups or inform us of our excessive speed, I saw flashing only the words, "GO RED SOX," and then, "COW-BOY UP!" This town of Brahmins (as opposed to brahmas) and hipper-than-thou college kids was making like so many Marlboro men, following the instigation of Millar to get tough, hang tough, be tough—tough as nails, tough as we need to be. The impetus had served us well in many an eighth and ninth inning that season, and would surely continue to do so (it was generally believed, in the New England neck of the woods).

Mr. Bachman, a lifelong resident of Boston and environs, took the back route to town. As we traveled over the hill and past the chapel at Boston College I began conjuring the memories of Jane's marriage to Steve in that country club over there, of climbing this hill during the Marathon when I ran as a bandit that one year, of trips like this to see the Sox, those hundreds of times. Dad never took this route in, but I had learned of it in 1976. The first time I drove him to a game this way, he was as amazed with my progress in life as he might've been if I were elected Massachusetts's junior senator. As we neared Kenmore, I shared these thoughts with Jane and her dad. "Lot of rich memories," Mr. Bachman said.

I fully anticipated adding one, this day.

The scene around the ballpark was much, much different than I remembered it from '75, '78, '86, or even '99. It used to be the Cask and Flagon, the Ark, and precious little else. Now there were a dozen bars, each with a line a block long. Evidently, the young adults—some of the car-turner-overs among them, no doubt—go to Kenmore as if to Mecca on Big Game Day, whether they have a ticket or not. They want to be near the fire, and I found this a little disturbing.

But, hey, we would be inside.

And then we were, in the auxiliary press box in right field. There were televisions out there that helped us interpret, via replay, what we had just seen happen—and still it was difficult to sort out the madness of that game. Certainly Pedro threw at Garcia's head. He was pitching lousy and first base was open. Certainly Clemens, who might well have thrown at Manny under these circumstances, did not do so, and certainly Manny overreacted. Certainly Zimmer lost his mind, whether because of his personal history with bean balls or because he hates the Red Sox to an insane degree. Certainly Clemens pitched wonderfully, and Jeter came up big (he should've had two, had Trot not robbed him). And we lost. Certainly, we lost. Under Stan's reckoning, the series was over.

In fact, though, the very craziness of that game seemed to kick-start the series. Let's face it, the first two games were a lot of things, but they weren't very exciting. Now, however, the Sox and Yanks were well and truly joined. "We expected a battle," said Grady. "Now it's a war." And Roger allowed, "I said it was going to be festive up here, but I didn't expect this festive."

That was a pretty good crack, and even as a Sox fan I appreciated it. All else I was interpreting differently, or so it seemed when I watched ESPN back at my sister's place in Wellesley and read the next day's papers (ours and theirs). The president of the Yanks said such "lawlessness" wouldn't happen in New York.

Pardon me?

In Boston, as developments continued, it seemed the lawlessness—which might even lead to criminal charges when the courts reopened after the Columbus Day holiday—involved those Yankees in the bullpen who left their cleat marks on the back of the grounds-crew guy. Sure, the guy was an idiot and shouldn't have cheered the Sox when working the Yanks' pen. But just as sure that smug Nelson has been an idiot his whole career (from our perspective) and was lying in wait for an opportunity to beat the crap out of someone. My sister, my wife, and I were agreed that Pedro should not be throwing at people's heads (see how clear-eyed we can be?) but as Mr. Bachman very reasonably said when he picked Jane and me up after the game, "They should have suspended Zimmer for the entire post-season." They certainly should have, no question. Coaches can't be charging star pitchers just because they're angry. And as for what happened to Zim, apparently the national media had it that a strong young athlete hammer-locked an old man, then threw him to the ground. I think *The Boston Globe* got it right: Pedro took Zimmer's energy and "tipped" him.

PERSPECTIVE, PERSPECTIVE, PERSPECTIVE. I started wondering if I could be objective about anything, at least while the suddenly incendiary series was progressing. Then

I found, by chance, that I could be. There was an article in the *Globe* about two guys getting suspended by WEEI radio—a guy with the last name of Dennis and a guy named Callahan. You Beantowners know them well because they're famous up there, and I had a suspicion at the time that I knew this Callahan. I asked my sister for some background, since the update article refused to mention the infamous remark that had led to the punishment. Turned out, these two drive-time guys had made a terrible, racist comment a short time previous, and the radio station had tried to overlook it because these guys had a big audience (and also probably because the radio station knew that racist remarks go down like ale in some parts of Boston). But the furor grew and finally WEEI suspended them for two weeks each for public pronouncements that might end a career in any other line of work.

"You know who the one guy is?" my sister asked. "He's that guy who used to write sports for the *Lowell Sun.*"

"Right. I knew I knew that name."

Gail explained that this guy—Callahan—now wrote for the *Herald* and moonlighted as the more conservative half of the good-old-boys duo on WEEI.

"I think he's in our high school hall of fame," I said to Gail. "Wonder what they think of the choice now."

Well, they probably weren't bothered by it. This is something Boston does sometimes that makes it hard to be as fervent a Boston fan as one might want to be. The city has a disturbing underbelly of racism, bigotry, insularity, and self-righteousness that does not compare favorably to some other cities' sense of self (am I talking about New York?). The busing brought it out years ago, but didn't end it. Almost every time I went up for a visit, there was something in the papers, or something in the air.

I wished I could ask Dad about the 'EEI flap. Yes, Dad grew more politically conservative as he got older but he never wavered on stuff like this. When we were playing home-run derby on Main Street in West Chelmsford as kids (clear the telephone wire and you can touch 'em all), everyone was in—fat kids, younger kids, unpopular kids, girls—because Dad insisted upon it. When his three children went to college, he and Mom were happy that we'd be meeting and making friends with people unlike those we'd known in Chelmsford. Dad was pretty sophisticated. In certain ways I think he was the smartest guy I ever knew.

GAIL, SCOTT, LUCI, and I talked about Gerry Callahan for a while as we watched the Pats beat the Giants on TV (every time we turned around that weekend, it was Boston-v-New York). The rain was coming down, and so we hadn't been able to get the kids into town as we'd hoped. We out-of-towners had had our hearts set on a Duck Boat tour for the kids—but, no, a washout.

That night's game was cancelled, too. The perspective in New York had it that this was a Bosox plot so we could realign our pitching and skip Burkett for now. But the way we heard it, the commissioner's office called off the game, just like it had called off beer sales in Fenway when things got ugly on the field on Saturday.

The Sunday rainout was the one that I had several seats for, and we had all garbed-up in Wellies and Macs and driven into town before the word came that the field was unplayable. Lucille, Gail, Scott, I, and young Thomas were approaching the ball park even as the fans started coming toward us, bearing the news, "Game's called." Thomas was Scott's nephew, an eleven-year-old shortstop and a rabid Nomar fan. When he had heard a few days earlier there might be a chance at a ticket, he had turned pleadingly to his mom, and she'd said okay. So Barbara (the mom), Thomas and Thomas's sister, Taylor, had piled into the car and begun the twelve-hour pilgrimage from Toledo. They were staying in one bedroom at Gail's house while my clan was in another. Gail and Scott's house was a hostel, or, even more, a tenement. This is what the post-season does to people. These are the kinds of situations the post-season creates.

We wandered Yawkey Way, trying to get something out

of that woebegone evening. We approached a gate and told the young woman that Thomas had come all the way from Toledo, and might he just go in and see the famous field? Finally the answer was yes (what would it have been in New York?) and Thomas met the Green Monster.

Outside, afterwards, we watched a few players depart. Walker's cute little daughter waved from the window of his SUV. Damon smiled as he drove off in his pickup (Damon was, at that moment, and as he would be a year later, hugely popular not only for bouncing back—that year, from his concussion—but for bouncing back with a hot bat, to boot). Then we went home, and Thomas approached his mother a second time.

"Okay, sure," said Barbara. "We'll stay another day."

"He's a good student," She explained to us. "One day won't matter."

I drove my family back to Westchester County on Columbus Day Monday, the beautiful fall foliage of Massachusetts and then Connecticut a balm after the recent frenzy. The rainout would cost me a contest. I'd watch Game Four on TV. Thomas, meantime, spent that Monday chillin'. He goofed around with Gail's kids, moistened and microwaved and shaped his brand new Bosox cap, put his game face on.

Then, finally, to Fenway, where he was transported by the 3-2 nail biter that turned Wakefield into a Beantown legend, and reinforced the opinion that Mussina is a hard luck loser (New York perspective) and/or soft (says me).

On Tuesday morning, I dropped by the office in mid-town to tie down a few things before heading for LaGuardia and, thence, Boston. I learned in Manhattan that I had no idea what was going on in the Series. My friend and colleague, Bob, a Yankees fan, said, "Hey, how's America's Team?" He was being sarcastic, but I didn't get it. He explained that the whole country now hated the Red Sox. He showed me the newspaper.

"Is that so?" I asked.

Or was that his perspective? (And the *Times*'.)

If it was so that we were now roundly reviled, how extraordinarily badly had we behaved to have accomplished this miracle, to have turned the general populace into fans of the thoroughly detestable Yankees (owned by George Steinbrenner, let's remember)?

Well, if it was so, then so be it. It was us against the world now, and if it went seven, then our headhunter would take the hill in Yankee Stadium on Thursday night against their headhunter, and we would stand behind ours. This thing was no longer pretty and it seemed it might get ugli-er, but it promised to be thrilling from there on in—no matter your perspective.

I had decided to fully enter the fray. I changed my look from ball fan to ranch hand. I had not only the will but the wherewithal to do so, because I'd spent most of 1992 on assignment in Australia, and had returned from Down Under with Coogi sweaters and koala dolls for family and friends, and a good deal of Outback garb for myself. The Stetson of Australia is called an Akubra, and while I was posted in Oz I bought a good, wide-brimmed one. It has a small, stylish feather. I picked up a Driza-bone riding coat that Clint Eastwood might envy, and I added to my collection of western-wear boots. Luci rarely allows me to go about Westchester in this stuff, but just then I was riding off to Beantown, where the rallying cry was Cowboy Up!

If the cabbie from Ernie's Taxi of Mount Kisco thought me strange, he kept it to himself, and for his discretion received a handsome tip upon delivering me to LaGuardia. I struggled getting my boots off and then back on at the X-ray machine, but nevertheless made the eleven-thirty shuttle after a sprint across the lobby. The fellow taking my ticket at the gate looked me over carefully, and then thought he got the gag. "Well, you sure are ready for Saddle Up!" I held my tongue. Yes, I could have cut this New York dolt with an indignant, "It's Cowboy Up!, fool." But the Sox had squared things at two games apiece, I was confident of our chances behind Derek and I was full of feelings of well being for my fellow man. "Yeah," I said to the buffoon. "Right."

The flight was smooth, and in a snap of the fingers I was back in the land of the Bosox where I belonged. On the cab ride in from Logan to the Pru Center I noticed that a sign redirecting traffic at one of the Big Dig work sites had been creatively altered. A graffiti artist with wit had taken his spray paint to the instruction "REVERSE CURVE," modifying it to "REVERSE THE CURSE."

Shortly on, after six or seven more blocks of Big Dig mess, I told the driver, "You can drop me right here."

Where would you meet to divvy up the ducats but at Legal Seafoods? Sister Gail, who works at Gillette, came down from the forty-seventh floor of the Pru Tower to join us, bearing the pair of Game Five tickets that she had scored. Her friend Millie arrived. She would sit alongside Gail in Section 8. I had the press pass plus four excellent seats in Section 13, several rows up but right behind first. I didn't necessarily want to sit in the auxiliary press section again, but realized that by doing so I could squeeze another friend into the park—and so I martyred. The Bag would be coming with Annie, and the other two seats would go to my lifelong friends from Chelmsford, Bruce and Mike (Larkin, this other Mike).

Mike and Bruce ordered Guinness. I had a bowl of the world's finest clam chowder, plus a Sam Adams. "Cowboy Up!" we toasted, as I handed out the tickets.

"Reverse the Curse!" someone added.

"Yeah," I said. "I read in the paper where David Wells actually believes in it. He said it was just one man's opinion, but he believes the Babe has cursed us and he's going to do his part to keep the Curse alive even though he hasn't pitched well in Fenway. He believes the Curse is real."

"You don't?"

"Well . . . no. Do you?"

There was a good deal of equivocation among these several college-educated, non-institutionalized adults. Finally I changed the subject. "What's with Gerry Callahan, anyway?"

"A shame upon Chelmsford," Mike answered.

"He made a mistake," said Bruce, who also had great sympathy at the time for Rush Limbaugh, as Rush headed in for treatment.

We enjoyed two rounds, and then started for the band-box. Walking up Comm Ave, we lamented the (long ago, now) demise of the Eliot Lounge, and talked about how spiffed up the brick townhouses looked. "When I was here in '76, college kids lived in them."

"Couldn't touch 'em now."

"Kinda sad," I said as we reached Kenmore Square.

The river of Bosox fans that streams through the Kenmore confluence on Game Day is always a shimmering, sublime organism. On Game Day Against the New York Yankees, ALCS tied 2-2, it was biblical in its glorious vibrancy and, by way of contrast, in its solemnity. It had in its flow the wide-eyed child, the rambunctious youth, the hopeful parent, the dread-filled pensioner, the helped-along grandmother. And, in this instance, at least one suburban cowboy from Westchester County, New York. "Can I borrow your hat?" asked an obviously-Boston University coed who had recently (and very obviously) been in proximity of a keg. Not today, sister. But by the way, where were you thirty years ago?

There was no question about it. As we settled into our seats, we felt that we were going to win this day. When Derek surfed the first on the shapely swell of only eight pitches, we were sure of it. He was on, we were on, the future was afoot. Old Dom DiMaggio had thrown a perfect strike to start things off with his ceremonial pitch, and everything had carried on from there. Tonight, we were convinced, Manny will go yard early and often, Nomar will break out, Trot and Todd will continue to do the things they've been doing this autumn, and then we will hand it over the Williamson, who's got as much mo as Mo. So what if Wells got us in the first? Now we're going to . . .

Issue a walk.

Another walk.

Oh, good, Boone.

0-2. Great.

Good, a grounder.

*Jeezus,* No!

So Derek was in the dugout holding his head in his

hands, and we were down—somehow—3-0. This was The Brutal Game, one of the most brutal I've ever experienced. It stayed 3-0 for so long, as Fenway sat with teeth clenched. Two men on and two outs and Nomar, who had batted .170 since Labor Day and had stunk—I mean, like bad cheese—throughout the post-season, gave us one of the worst at-bats in baseball history, fanning on a belt-high fastball that the-Nomar-we-once-knew would take to the Monster seats. Nomar courageously walked a few innings later to load 'em up, and Manny immediately trickled one to . . . Boone. (After the game, the batting coach of the Sox would applaud—*applaud*—Nomar's two bases-on-balls.) Manny did homer once, but with the bases clear, rather than filled. And Nomar got his first RBI in the postseason in the eighth. But here's how: Mo came in and the Recently Great Todd Walker gave us hope by belting one down to right that nearly went out. It wound up being a triple. Nomar grounded out—*way to go!*—and Walker scored. My friend Scoggins of the *Sun*, the official scorer for the Sox, sound-ed desultory when he announced Nomar's RBI to the assembled press.

I had been in Nomar's corner ever since I saw him at Trenton and then watched him assemble a legion of young fans in Beantown. Kids should have their heroes. And also, Dad had been a Nomar guy, so it was my job to root as Dad would have rooted. Dad no longer could, so I was required to. But, frankly, the *me* side of me was now thinking that Nomar should just pack up and go to California if, as he said, he didn't like playing in front of all these people, with all this pressure and attention. He should go there with Mia and start to enjoy life again. Because he was no longer helping us in Boston, where we were late in Game Five, losing, the Yanks batting under .200 for the series and about to go up three games to two. I was down on Nomar, down on Pedro, down on Manny. Give me Todd and Trot and Tim and a teamful of guys like that. I'd take Derek, too, who Cowboyed Up after that mess in the second, and got us deep into this game. To scant avail.

Down in Section 8, the cotton-candy guy was giving cotton candy away for free. Millie said to Gail, "Well, no more games till April."

Gail, a good, solid fan, reflected upon several facts: that it's not over till it's over, that there will be another game tomorrow in New York no matter the outcome of this one, and that the shelf life of cotton candy must be at least a month. She said, "We could still play here Saturday night. The World Series. Why's he giving up?!"

Later, she said to me forlornly, "I just don't know why they can never win. You just sit there in the stands, watching, wondering."

We were back at her place at that point. She had put out cheese and crackers and Sam Adams for Millie, Annie, and the guys. Not everyone got back out to Wellesley. Some didn't feel like socializing.

But others did, and we munched and sipped as Gail and Scott's kids, along with Millie's daughter, ran amok till way past their bedtimes. Bag and I recounted yet again how we had scored tickets to the Bucky Dent game almost precisely a quarter-century ago, and told other sad jokes that gradually built context for The Brutal Game. Then Bag and Annie bid us adieu, and I repaired to the couch to nurse my wounds and my nightcap. Slowly, I got into the Cubs-Marlins game that was on the tube. The camera kept scanning the smiling, happy, giddy people in Wrigley Field, and I had conflicting emotions.

*Good for them!*

*Why them, and not us?*

I had been so deep into Sox-Yanks for a week now, I had barely realized that the Cubs had gotten themselves to the verge. And there they were.

"What's the score?" Gail asked.

"Three-zip."

"Inning?"

"Eighth."

"Prior still pitching."

"Yeah. He's tremendous."

"Well, good for them. I'm going to bed. You switch off the lights?"

"Sure."

My sister went upstairs, and I was alone with the final ballgame of a long day. Over the next several minutes, as I slouched, holding my glass on my stomach, lifting it occasionally to my lips, I watched a fan catch a ball in the left-field stands, a shortstop boot a grounder, Prior turn into a pumpkin, the Marlins score eight runs, and the collective visage of the Wrigleyites turn into one which has just witnessed something concocted by Stephen King (who had, by the way, failed in his efforts to de-hex Fenway only hours earlier. It has been a very spooky day all 'round). Now my emotions were even more conflicted than before.

*Good God.*

*Poor kid—not his fault.*

*That shortstop's as big a dog as Nomar.*

*And I thought our game was Brutal.*

*Well, they're at home and they've got flame-throwing Kerry Wood going tomorrow, and we'll be back in Yankee Stadium and we've got . . .*

John Burkett, who I understand is a fine bowler in his spare time.

I was unhappy with myself, my misery, and especially my lack of charity. It seemed that if we couldn't win it all—or at least beat the Yankees—I didn't want the Cubbies to win, either. I didn't understand that Curse of the Billy Goat thing, but if we can't shake the Bambino, why should they be able to shed their goat? Let the world get Yanks-Marlins, and I hope the ratings crash through the floor. Hey, best of all: Let the Marlins win.

I was, at that point, it does not need to be said, in a thoroughly foul mood. I went to bed after the carnage in Chicago had ended, and awoke the next morning to a torrential downpour of rain that reflected the state of all baseball affairs (as I was seeing them). My sister drove me to Logan, and I suffered a suitably bumpy flight down to New York. The stiff wind was probably blowing straight out at the Stadium, and would no doubt lift a couple of Bernie or Nick or Derek jacks later in the day.

Work was slow, and then at three thirty I hopped the D Train for the Bronx along with Bob—friend, colleague, Yankee fan. I had those two seats in the bleachers again, and I figured if I didn't offer Bob one today—his pinstripe loyalty notwithstanding—then he wouldn't get to see a game. What a sport I am.

So, Game Six. We began it in Stan's bar, and were still there, since the bleacher line across the street was extensive, when Giambi hit his first-inning homer off our semipro bowler. The saloon exploded in excitement. Bob was truly sympathetic. "This must be hard for you."

"Brutal," I admitted. "Just brutal. Game Five was brutal. This is brutal." We finished our beers and headed for the stadium. Bob seemed to have a spring in his step. I felt mean again, and expressed it thusly: "That shot sure looked steroid-juiced to me."

In Section 57, I was still keeping my Red Sox affiliation under wraps, but I was not into the games-playing with my neighbors that enlivened Game One for me. When the Sox went meekly in the second, I offered to Bob, "I'm miserable. You know, the only thing this club did all year was hit. And the only thing they haven't done a bit of in this series is hit."

In the third inning, they started to hit. Even against Andy Pettite, who's pure money, they started to hit. Varitek hit it a mile. Nomar got a hit, even though it wasn't much of a hit. "He's on his one-base-at-a-time recovery program," I said to Bob. I was tense. Hoping. And then, quickly and stunningly, just as suddenly as the Yanks had gone up 3-0 against Lowe in Boston, the Sox were ahead 4-1.

Then Grady gave it back, sticking with the bowler way too long in the fourth. Five-four Yanks, then 6-4 when they added a run in the fifth. We were using young Arroyo and barely-on-the-roster Jones. They weren't getting nailed, but they were getting nicked.

In the sixth, something interesting developed. Two Yanks on, one out. Double steal, second and third. Giambi up, first base suddenly open. "Do you walk him?" Bob asked me.

"I know he hit the homer," I said. "But I think you pitch to him." Embree struck him out magnificently. "I do hope that proves significant," I said. Bernie followed with a hot ground-out to third.

In the sixth Contreras, the Cuban whom the Yanks stole from us in the off-season, struck out the side with that nasty split-finger fastball of his. We're doomed, I figured. They've finally found their bridge to Rivera.

Nomar, who earlier had booted the ball that led to the four runs, thus prompting his goat horns to grow longer at a Pinocchioan pace, was in the dugout figuring he liked the look of that split about as much as I did. So he said to himself, *Whatever he throws me first, I go after. I can't let him get to his out-pitch.* What Jose threw was a slider, and his next pitch to Manny was a fastball. Two pitches into the seventh inning and the Red Sox had sent spheroids a cumulative 820 feet, the wind helping them accelerate as they zoomed over Bernie's head in center. Ortiz's hot shot hit the first base bag—we were hitting, and we were getting lucky, too—and suddenly we were tied. Mr. Torre elected to walk Varitek intentionally to load the bases, and his reliever Heredia elected to walk Damon on four more pitches, handing the Red Sox a 7-6 lead. "This," I said to Bob, "is the great game this series has been waiting for." He appeared to think otherwise.

It was madness at the Stadium, 56,000 disbelieving fans watching plastic bags whip around in the whirlwind—make that maelstrom—56,000 fans screaming, desperately, for their boys to come back. *I paid 200 bucks to be here and I want to see the celebration!* But Embree, Timlin, and Williamson were doing a fair impression of the Nelson, Stanton, Rivera act of old—eerily familiar, in these confines—and the Yankees would be denied that night. Trot added two with a mighty blow in the ninth—third deck, way up, deep right field—and there it was: nine to six, but just as important, sixteen hits by our side. We were hitting again.

Would we hit Clemens tomorrow?

Yes, I reflected on the train ride home, everything is in place. Game Seven, Roger's last game, Pedro's redemption . . . Too bad, I thought later as I watched the Marlins prevail on the tube, too bad the Cubbies won't be joining us. Weren't those fans smiling, ever so recently? Ah, the vicissitudes of fate. Of life.

Thursday dawned lover-ly; it was a crisp and clear and somewhat calmer day, a perfect day for baseball or anything at all. Ernie Banks, were he still swinging the bat, would choose to play two on such a day. But Mr. Cub and all things Cubby were yesterday's news, and this day was about Sox-Yanks, a historic twenty-sixth meeting in a single season (Yanks ahead 13-12; about two-thirds of the contests thrillers). It was about Pedro-Roger redux, probably with a chin-music *leitmotif*. "It's every kid's dream," according to the Sox' Embree, who had slain the Argonaut Jason so heroically the previous evening. "You sit in your backyard growing up and you dream up these kind of match-ups in your head, a showdown between two Hall-of-Fame-caliber guys."

According to Theo, wunderkinder GM of these Bosox, it was fate and destiny, dancing a tango, "We've been on a collision course for a hundred years. It's definitely appropriate, definitely meant to be, and certainly poetic. It's special for both franchises, regardless of the result." Obviously Yale.

The sage Mr. Torre, who has never struck me as the mystical type, allowed merely, "I guess it was supposed to come down to this."

No fewer than five different folks involved with the ongoing fracas that was that series, including a manager, a GM, and a few players, were quoted in the morning sports pages in echo, "It doesn't get any better than this."

At the school bus stop, young Reed and I shared a handshake and a pledge, that our friendship would endure whatever might transpire at the Stadium in twelve hours. I handed over the ticket stub from Game Six, and he thanked me for the souvenir. Then he and Caroline, who had finally told me only that morning that she was officially a Red Sox fan (she had been taunting her dad, as six-year-olds do), gave me a kiss and boarded the bus. Reed, in that Yankee shirt of his, went west, and I, in my Bosox cap, turned east and hoofed it down to the train station. What would the day bring for both of us? For Stan, too—Hi Stan, I waved—and for the folks up in Massachusetts—Gail, Scott, Millie, Bag, Annie, Mike, Bruce—and the fellow exiles down here like Jane. The traitors like New Hampshire-native Mike. For anxious Thomas of Toledo, who never forsook his Nomar . . . What would it bring, for all of us?

At the office, work had little to do with work. I began by fielding the many emails and voicemails left the previous night by other citizens of Red Sox Nation. (A representative excerpt, this from Bruce: "Gentlemen, in Latin, the translated phrase is 'the thing speaks for itself.' A day ago, we were in mourning. Tonight, a different tale. Anyone wonder about the strength of the winds, and the demeanor of the sky all day? I looked at it as a cleansing of all that had taken place in the past. I say New England is due. Anything can and will happen in Game Seven. I say, bring it on. It's the middle of October and the Yankee fans are still worried—how about that? If security allows the game to take place, Pedro will rule, Wake will save, and destiny will be fulfilled. God Bless America! Red Sox Nation, sleep well. Battle looms. Be courageous and unafraid. The Yankees do not suck, in fact, but they are beatable! Go SOX!" And this from Bag: "I can see and hear it now at the victory celebration at City Hall Plaza a week from next Monday. After first trooping out for the crowd's adulation—to the tune of

'When the Saints Come Marching In'—Pesky and DiMaggio from '46, Yaz, Scottie, and Lonborg from '67, Carlton, Rice, Evans, Lynn, and Luis from '75, Bruce and (again) Dewey and Jimbo from '86, and after a moment of silence for all who could and should have lived long enough to see this day, but especially Ted, Ned Martin, and Ken Coleman, each of whom would have been there if the same event had happened in '99, when it should have, the crowd welcomes this year's heroes as Bing sings, 'Fairy Tales Can Come True . . .'"

Obviously I agreed with all sentiments, in these missives and the many others. I did get a queasy feeling about the wisdom of putting such predictions on paper—or even out there in cyberspace.

My bleacher mate for the ultimate game would finally be my ultimate partner and beloved wife. Having lost that earlier chance to the rainout, she now enjoyed a second opportunity—just like Pedro. Luci and I rode the subway up to the Bronx. I was still in my Cowboy Up duds, minus the telltale ten-gallon hat.

Section 57 was a tense place, and juiced to a degree it hadn't been during the three previous games in the Bronx. My beefy pal arrived and I introduced him to my wife, learning finally that his name was Billy.

There's no need to recap the game. You know how it unfolded. As for us, our evening was, for the longest time, not only tolerable but also enjoyable. As opposed to The Brutal Game, this one was a delight—our guys on top, Pedro cruising, Clemens clocked, not an exciting game but moving toward a thrilling denouement, for perhaps we were indeed going to . . .

I don't believe in curses, as you know, but is it interesting that the last time Lucille was by my side at a post-season baseball game was Game Six of the 1986 World Series in Shea, as we both gazed in awe when a ball went directly through our first baseman and wound up in right field?

In any event, yes, sure, Grady left Pedro in much, much too long, and I told Luci that Grady was doing so even as he was doing it. But then, someone had to leave him in too long, or make some other equally egregious mistake. Right?

In the ninth, Luci and I weren't feeling well, and we knew pretty much how it would end. Harley-shirted Billy still didn't know I was a Red Sox fan, and genuinely commiserated when I told him that, hey, when you bring the wife, you've got to free up the nanny by one o'clock (which was true). What can you do? I said to Billy. We shook hands. He asked if I'd be there for the series. He meant the World Series. The Yanks were there already, the way he saw it—and the way I saw it, too. I told Billy, my friend, that I just didn't know. I just did not know.

We were heading up the Saw Mill River Parkway, maybe about White Plains, when Boone hit the homer. I thought of Dad. I hoped he wasn't watching. Perhaps the car slowed a bit, but there was not even enough energy in this particular fan to issue an expletive. And besides, this had already happened, hadn't it? Didn't this happen five minutes or an hour ago? Somewhere? And only now it was manifesting itself on the field of play? Dad had already seen this, hadn't he?

On the radio they were talking about the game as the most dramatic post-season win in the history of the Yankee franchise, because of all that attended it—the Sox, Pedro, the comeback, the finish. Maybe it was that. Who knows? Who cares?

My lovely Caroline, finally committed to the team at age six and, God bless her, for a lifetime, had asked me that morning to open her door and tell her who won, no matter how late I got home. I walked upstairs with Luci at 1:20 a.m., still feeling numb, beat up, very tired. I was trying to remember, as I climbed the stairs, how I had answered when Caroline had made her request. Had I told her, Oh, Sweetie, I'll fill you in tomorrow? Or did I promise to open her door and whisper in her ear?

I walked past her bedroom, leaving her be. Spare her this day. She has plenty of time to be a Sox fan.

ONE CRUCIAL NIGHT during the off-season, Curt Schilling went on the Red Sox superfans' website, the Sons of Sam Horn, which was run by a bunch of guys whose fanaticism put even the BLOHARDS to shame. Schilling monitored the chat for a while, then he typed in some words introducing himself. They doubted him. They put before him a slate of challenging questions to which only Schilling would know the answers. Finally convinced, the Bosox boosters stayed up all night long, trying to coax the big guy into joining our crusade. Schilling's a man who, apparently, enjoys a crusade. The next day, acting as his own agent, he signed a two-year deal with the Red Sox for a little more than twelve million dollars a year, with an option for a third-year that would kick in if the Red Sox won the World Series. Such a clause, based upon team performance, was illegal under Major League Baseball rules—gamblers could always offer an athlete even more than the option to throw a crucial game in crunch time. But the idea of Schilling entering the Sox-Yankee wars must have seemed so exciting to everyone involved, the illicit clause slid right by the commissioner's office.

At his signing Schilling was handed, and then held up for the photographers, a T-shirt emblazoned with the phrase YANKEES SUCK. I saw the picture in the papers the next day and thought to myself, *Hey, this could be interesting.*

AS SCHILLING RACKED up his major-league-leading twenty-one regular season wins, I mowed, planted, raked, hit tennis balls, built bookshelves, took the kids to the beach, and attended nary a ballgame. You couldn't touch a ticket all year in Fenway without pulling strings. And at ages four, four, and six, the kids were, I still felt, just a bit young for the hostility their B-hats would engender at Yankee Stadium.

I planned to do the post-season from home, too—I really did. I was going to sit in front of the tube with Luci and the gang, imparting to the twins the reasons for the Red Sox, reasons that Caroline now understood clearly. Then I would coax the kids to go upstairs with Mom after an inning or two, and watch the rest of the debacle by myself. I said to myself, and perhaps aloud to Luci, that I was going to approach the post-season this way because the children were now four, four, and six, and I wanted to spend some baseball time with them. But, really, I was going to do it differently—in front of the tube, rather than in the arena—because I thought a small-screen experience might mitigate the pain.

And, of course, there would be pain.

Oh, I hadn't given up on the team. It was rather that, after 2003, how could I reasonably assume they might pull it off? And even if, in dreams, I did assume that, why would I put myself, on the eve of a fifty-first birthday, through the ordeal again—another weeklong month-long? journey into madness? No, I sure wasn't going to do that a second time (a third, counting '86). When this year's Grady moment occurred, I would be in a place where I could sip the last of my beer, hit the clicker, and trudge to bed. I would not be in the bleachers in the Bronx with my lovely wife, watching incredulously as my manager leaves the mound, and leaves Pedro where he is.

And then, just like the year before, tickets started falling from the sky. My friend, Eddie, at Major League Baseball had some that I could get for cost. Gail and Scott landed some for Fenway. The Bag had an extra or two.

What are you going to do?

"Honey, what do you say we take the kids up to Bean-town for Columbus Day weekend. We can stay with Gail. The foliage will be nice. Maybe take Friday off and we can get a jump on it." (And oh, say, by the way, Hon, lookee here. There's a game against California that night! Whaddya know?!)

So we dropped off Daisy at the vet's, picked up the kids early at school, and pointed the green Sienna north-north-east once more, Boston-bound.

The drive through Connecticut and, then, eastern Massachusetts on a gleaming Friday midday was glorious. So was the event in prospect. Gail and Scott had made the offer that cannot be refused—"We'll put the kids to bed"— so my date for this four o'clock start would again be my bride. We took the T into town, walked through the throng outside the park, and entered Fenway. I immediately felt the charge, and it was a most familiar frisson. A packed ball-park, particularly in the post-season, obviously generates tremendous energy. But the shiver I shivered was the same one I had shivered every night of the hundred or so when I climbed to the empty bleachers during my college years in the '70s, the same one I'd felt when my brother and I went to the Ted game, the same one twelve months ago in this park, which I hadn't seen since then. I get a certain feeling on an ocean beach in the off-season, another on a moun-taintop in New Hampshire, another at Fenway—each and every time.

The field-box seats that Dad had bought circa 1960 probably cost a dollar and a quarter and I know that the bleacher seats that I bought in 1975 went for a buck twen-ty-five. This night, in 2004, our box seats in deep right, which for most of Fenway's nine decades had been sold as grandstand, were ninety dollars per. But no matter. We were here, we had Sam Adamses in hand, and the Sox were tak-ing the field. Life, at the moment, was very good indeed.

Luci knew what it meant to me, and gave my knee a squeeze.

"I like six-oh leads," I casually remarked when the lead got to six-oh. "I can take one of these." My neighbor to the right, a baseball-head of deep wisdom and evident experience, said, "It's not over." Well, of course, it wasn't. Nevertheless, I said to Luci, "I guess Gail won't get her game in tomorrow." I had the same seats for Saturday, and it had already been arranged that, should the Sox, who were already ahead two games to none in the best-of-five series, require four games to dismiss the Angels, Gail would accompany me to the next set-to. I sensed that my neighbor shot me a glance when I voiced the notion that baseball matters versus the Californians were pretty much wrapped up. More on that shortly.

The Angels got a run, then another, as three different Sox pitchers yielded some chippy hits and walked three enemy batsmen in the seventh. When you're way ahead you don't want to be giving free passes, but the Sox were obliging. Now, the presumptive and eventual American League Most Valuable Player, Vlad Guerrero, was stepping in, and Mike Timlin's lanky presence on the mound inspired little confidence in this particular camper. "You know," I said to Luci, "If Francona's already decided he's going to use Foulke tonight, he could bring him in here and stop this nonsense. Never let the Angels get off the snide." She smiled at me. I might as well have been speaking Martian. Timlin stayed in, the ball went out, the 6-6 score went up on the Green Monster scoreboard and all available oxygen fled the Fens.

It was two full innings before the crowd learned to cheer again. During this time of enforced quiet, I discussed with my neighbors whether the Sox had ever blown a lead in a crucial game, then come back to win. Our analysis dated back only to 1946, but we figured they hadn't. They'd blown plenty of big leads in crucial games, but had always come to a sad end.

"You jinxed them, you know," the fellow two seats down said. "It's your fault. That stuff about 'No game tomorrow.' For a baseball guy, that wasn't too bright."

I was, of course, contrite. The last thing the Boston franchise needed was extra hexing, large or small. The Curse of the Bambino, after all. *(Was I starting to believe in it? Could David Wells have been right?* Two thousand and three had acted upon me in strange and disquieting ways.)

I gazed out upon the field, and watched the ninth-inning rally come to nothing. "Hey, honey," I said to Luci. "How many ballgames have we been to together?"

"Including the minors?"

"No, just Sox."

"This is probably the third or fourth."

"And two of them were the sixth game of the '86 World Series, when they collapsed against the Mets, and the seventh game against the Yanks last year—right? The Grady/Pedro/Boone game."

"That would be right."

"Honey," I said, "You've got to be the world-record-holder for most-inconceivable-Red-Sox-folds-per-games-attended." I half wondered whether Luci was bringing her own curse. "Maybe you should stop coming." I wasn't serious. Of course I wasn't. She's my wife, after all.

Francona did use Foulke, and then Lowe, who had been sentenced to the bullpen after his poor season. Derek, of whom I was a fan, survived a shaky, scary inning. "Hey," I said at this point, "look who's warming up with Percival for California." It was good old Jared Washburn, the losing starter from Game One. "Wonder what that's about?"

We found out in the eleventh, when the dynamic K-Rod finally tired and the Angels skip, Mike Scioscia, apparently devoted beyond common sense to the idea of lefty-lefty, brought Washburn in to face Big Papi. "A starter walking into this situation, 35,000 nutcases going nuts, and the Angels could be done with Percival unused in the bullpen?" I said aloud. "I don't know about this one."

One pitch later, we all knew, as Ortiz's mighty swat propelled the ball high, then higher. When it finally came down it did so in the seats atop the Monster. The celebration at Fenway would last more than an hour. For my part,

I was off the hook. I said to my neighbor as I hugged my wife, "Hey, piece-a-cake!"

The next day, with no game on, we took the kids for a stroll on the dunes of Crane's Beach in Ipswich, then for fried clams at Farnum's. It was good to be up here in Massachusetts. Every third person, and everyone in our party, was wearing a Bosox cap and/or T-shirt. Back in New York in any given October, but particularly in the last two, I only felt comfortable when among BLOHARDS. Up here in the Bay State, by contrast—putting down a plateful of good Ipswich clams, chasing them with fine Ipswich Ale— I was at home, and content.

I guess I rooted for the Yankees that weekend. I knew they were going to take the Twins anyway, so why not put on the bravest face and declare it's better to go through the Yanks.

I wondered as I drove the family south-southwest on a beautiful Columbus Day morn if that had been the right way to think.

TICKETS KEPT FALLING like the foliage-season leaves, and Tuesday night found me and my former *Sports Illustrated* colleague and longtime friend, Craig Neff, side-by-side, high above first base in two more ninety-dollar seats. We discussed our winning week in the *SI* football pool (we're in our silver anniversary season as a team. Time does fly). We talked about our families, the war, the election. And then we settled in for the game. As the Yanks surged to a huge lead (6-0, 7-0, with Mussina working on a perfect game), we fell back into discussion of the election, the war, our families, our winning week in the *SI* football pool. "It's going to take a Mussina Inning to get us back into this one," I said.

And then, lo, there was the Mussina Inning. It is truly astonishing how quickly things unravel for that guy. One minute, he's perfection. Within seconds, he has given up four hits to five batters and is being saved from himself by Mr. Torre.

It turned out Tom Gordon really did have a tired arm, and with one-hundred-year-old Paul Quantrill cooked by overuse in midsummer, the Yankee bullpen, short of Mariano, was an unimposing organism. The Sox kept chipping away and when Papi sent a Ruthian shot to deep, deep left, Yankee Stadium felt much as Fenway had when Vlad went yard. (It felt that way except to me, of course. At that moment, I was feeling rather peppy.) Ortiz's shot did not get out; it glanced off Matsui's glove. So instead of being tied at eight, the Yanks were clinging to a one-run lead, with our big guy parked at third—where he would idle till inning's end.

Rivera would get the save tonight, and that was something approaching okay with me. His nephew, said to be like a son to him, had, only days prior, been electrocuted in Mariano's native Panama. Two had died, in fact. The boy's father had tried to save the boy after a mishap at a swimming pool, and had become a second victim. Mariano had returned only that night from the funerals to "do my job." On such a night, you do not begrudge such a man his success against you.

It's unfortunate, but I'd always felt that it was hard to properly hate a Torre-edition Yankee team, what with men like Rivera, Jeter, Williams, and Posada—and, formerly, O'Neill, Brosius, Tino, even Sojo. I mean, I *had* hated them, as I had managed to hate the Yankees while still cheering for Mickey Mantle in my boyhood—but it had often been hard. If Torre and Cashman had made it easier for us lately with the addition of cheaters like Giambi and crumbums like Lofton and Sheffield, they still retained those classy veterans, Rivera principal among them. My feelings, then, at the end of Game One: Let us allow a day or two of sympathy to prevail for Mariano. Maybe by the weekend we'll be ready to curse him anew.

In a Proper Bostonian way, of course.

Boston is, as I mentioned when discussing Dennis and

Callahan's transgressions earlier, a town with storied racial strife, and elitism deep in its DNA. As such, it should make no claim on moral superiority when regarding any other city, least of all the successful melting pot that is New York. But when you have a rooting interest one way or the other, you're allowed to be entertained by your opposition's boorishness. (Entertained, I should point out, not by any unsavory japes themselves, but by the sheer boobosity of those who make them.) Early in the evening, Craig and I had been amused and appalled to overhear two lugs three rows in front debate whether the truly vile metaphor that one of them had applied to Ortiz was beyond the pale, or just within the bounds of ballpark etiquette. Later, when Matsui, who at the time already had five RBIs in a game that the Yanks would win by three (Timlin would stink again, yielding two in the eighth), came to bat in the ninth, a belcher in back of me, recalling only that Hideki had not made the tough catch on Ortiz's fly, suggested he "fall on his sword." Charming.

As I say, we did not win. Worse, the reason we did not win was that Curt Schilling, the crucial cog in a team that was purpose-built for the post-season, lasted only three innings. Why was Schilling shelled so? Because a persistent ankle injury that had been exacerbated in Game One versus California was re-tweaked when he was walking up the dugout steps to the field. Yes, correct. As he was about to take the mound and stay nose-to-nose with Mussina until the Mussina Inning, something caused the tendon to fray further.

Something.

*The Bambino. Surely it was the Bambino.*

Before moving on from Game One, I must brag. That night featured my first-ever called shot. During the Sox uprising, Jason was about to get his licks. The Yanks fans were tensing. Varitek's a player, even if he had been dreadful at the plate in Yankee Stadium that year. Our switch-hitter was batting from the south side, and he has power from there. Our Boston team was looking for their leader to lead. Tall, tall Tanyon Sturtze was on the mound, and he could bring it from on high. His first pitch was a beautiful ninety-five-mile-per-hour fastball, and it was *steeerike* one. I digested all of the above. Each item had been factored in when I turned to the young boy on my right—eleven years old, maybe twelve—and said, "This guy's oh-for-thirty-four in this ballpark now. That guy's certainly bringing the heat again. This guy's a veteran and knows heat. That guy wants to be a hero. This guy wants to break out. See that sign?" I pointed to the yellow one just east of the bullpen in right. "Five rows up." Tanyon brought, Jason swung. *Bam!* I was wrong. Four rows behind the sign.

But, yes, we lost.

The *Times* headline on the morning after read "Here

We Go Again," and when I saw it I realized, *Yeah, it had been a helluva game. The untouchable Mussina, the roaring comeback, the dramatic appearance of Rivera. Would Chapter Two measure up?*

It certainly arrived fraught with possibility. Central to this was Pedro, great pitcher, headhunter, Yankees' punching bag. After his second straight drubbing by the Yanks near season's end, Pedro had famously issued what was (we Sox fans knew) a characteristically cryptic and, well, crazy declaration. He had suggested that the big fellows in pinstripes were, just possibly, "my daddy." *Hmmm.* So then, might the stadium chant "Nine-teen, eigh-teen; Nine-teen, eigh-teen!" be joined by, or even supplanted by, something new tonight?

"Who's your daddy?!"

"Who's your daaaddy?!"

*"Who's your daaaaaaddy!?!?!?!?!"*

Thunderous is the only word to describe it. And, clearly, there was only one way to silence it. Pitch well. Pedro took the mound, walked a guy, hit a guy, looked awful, jammed the bases, gave up a run—then twirled like a magician, and got out of the inning without further damage. How? I can't remember. The whole thing was a mess, but there it was.

Second inning, Pedro crafty. Third, Pedro stronger. Fourth, Pedro in charge. "That's it," I said silently, being a proponent of the current wisdom vis-à-vis Pedro. "Ride this horse to Pitch Number One Hundred, then go straight to the pen." I was sure that Francona, in Year One of the Bosox AGL (After Grady Little), shared this philosophy and would do as directed.

He did not, and that was why it wasn't a 1-1 game going into the ninth, but 3-1 Yanks. John Olerud, whose power was yesteryear, hit a two-run homer off Pedro on pitch one hundred and five, and what was a very good game (especially for New York hurler Jon Lieber) was not a great one.

What else do I recall from Game Two? Not much. There was this guy beneath the stands whose face had been pummeled and who was catching his dripping blood in a beer cup. The usual. Mariano got another save, and that was okay with me. We were heading back to Fenway. We'll kill 'em in Game Three.

IN THE PRESENT-DAY SOX-YANKS conflicts, whether the game is close or a blowout, you kill or get killed. Each game is a killer. In Game Three, we really got killed. We got trounced in historic, emotionally devastating fashion. All of the statistics, from hits to time-elapsed to pitchers-used, was the most this, the biggest that, the longest this, the worst that—ever. One fact should suffice: nineteen was the most runs ever scored in a post-season game by the Yankees, who've played a few post-season games through the years. Every Red Sox pitcher was Timlin tonight, including Timlin. Things got off to a bad start right from the start with the starter, young Bronson, who had recently dazzled against the Angels. *The Yankees aren't the Angels, Master Arroyo, and welcome to the true playoffs.* The only Boston pitcher to acquit himself was Wakefield, who took one for the team, volunteering to chew up some innings with his floater, meantime sacrificing his scheduled start. That is an old-school ballplayer.

Other thoughts about Game Three? None. Even now, I don't want to think about it. That Cowsills performance before the game was ridiculous. The Cowsills? *They'll sure get the juices flowing, eh?* I don't want to talk about it. Can't believe they're still alive—the Cowsills. Come on, Dr. Charles, what was that about?

In looking retrospectively for any good news at all beyond Wakefield's martyrdom, I do remember that, when Mendoza balked home a run, I said to myself, *Well, at least I'm not at home watching FOX. At least I don't have to hear Professor McCarver explain to me the history of the balk and why, generally, it's not a good idea to balk in the sport of baseball with a man on third.*

The game had been so bad, and had delivered the Sox so emphatically to the brink, that it not only allowed but it forced those of us in the ballpark to think about anything but the horrid baseball before us. We talked about better days. We did some catching up.

"Took me all these years to pay you back!" So said Jake—the eternal Bag, my college buddy—who had put me in that particular ninety-dollar seat behind third on that particular night. Apparently I had done him a similar if less-costly favor during some bygone post-season—'86, must have been—and the fact had sat there in his Red Sox brain until he could reciprocate, which he was finally able to do in the '04 ALCS.

The whole evening reeked of reminiscence for me. It was a journey through the past, even unto the finality of an important and dispiriting Sox loss. Examples: Jake had arranged to meet behind the left-field foul pole, as had been our tradition in the late '70s when he and I, both post-grad students in Boston at the time, routinely cut night classes to follow those very good Red Sox teams from a center-field vantage. Now, in '04, we compared notes during the debacle at hand about those better, bygone games—"Remember the twin 4-0 twi-night wins over (was it?) Minnesota, Tiant, and (was it?) Reggie Cleveland winning, fog so thick, we couldn't see home plate?" We freshened a friendship that, despite the separation enforced by distance and family, needed no sprucing up.

"Have you eaten?" Jake asked in, maybe, the sixth, as he went for beers and whatever else.

"I have," I answered. Had I ever.

I had dined before the game at Clio's with Gail and Scott, who also had tickets for Fenway that night. Gail, Scott, and I sat at the bar and enjoyed the most extraordinary sushi I had ever eaten, Manhattan sushi included. Gail said that *Boston* magazine had recently tried to pin the *frou-frouing* of Beantown cuisine—smaller portions, preciousness of presentation—on Clio's, but then had given up the effort, as Clio's was so simply and dauntingly excellent. Scott sipped his Beefeater's martini (he had, in the past couple of years, adopted our dad's brand), and tried a piece of Kobe beef with salt. Gail and I talked about Dad and all those Sox games with Dad, and she apologized for not taking me to a more appropriately "baseball" restaurant before the game.

"Gail," I said. "We're in the Eliot Hotel. This space used to be the Eliot Lounge. Spaceman came here after almost every game. That bar was Marathon headquarters. Tommy Leonard—he poured me more pints than . . . Well, I can't tell you what good bones this place has!" And then I tried the raw tuna thingie in the coconut juice.

Between Clio's and a nightcap of Maker's Mark in Jake's living room in Andover at two in the morning, there was that awful game. Even the next morning, the taste of it—and, well, maybe of Clio's and the bourbon, too—was in my mouth. I asked the Bag and Annie if there was a nice jogging route nearby, where a Sox fan might clear his head and sweat away some sins.

The run, it turned out, furthered the resonant reverie I had sunk into. I trotted down Chestnut Street and hung a right into the bird sanctuary owned by Phillips Andover Academy, the famous prep school. Large maples and pines shaded the needled pathway. These were the woods of my youth—Merrimack Valley woods—which Luci and I were trying to approximate for our kids by choosing Westchester County, which is about as New Englandy as you can get while remaining in the Apple's orbit. The foliage in Andover was just about peak. It reflected on the pond down below, just through the grove.

I exited the sanctuary and beheld the campus. I ran up and into it. It was so very Phineas, so John Knowles. (Do kids still read that? Will mine?) Near the main road, which yet had no cars stirring, I loped past the Andover Inn. My family, before my father's death, had a tradition of going to New England inns for a pre-Christmas Christmas dinner. One year, on the twenty-second or twenty-third of December, we had come here. Dad had really enjoyed that night, and I thought it was because, as a product of Lowell and its Lowell High School, he had long been aspirational about things like Andover. Andover and such as Andover, those were the dreams. Now, there he was, in his seniority, able to dine with his wife and children at the Andover Inn, on the grounds of Phillips Andover Academy. I'll bet he felt positively patriarchal that evening.

As I jogged out over the playing fields, I was thinking about how I wished I could tell Dad about Clio's—"Remember the Eliot Lounge? Bill Lee usta go there?"—and that Gail and I had enjoyed a fine meal there before a Sox-Yanks game. He would have thought, *How can they afford that?* Then he might have felt pretty good about himself and Mom.

Red Sox Nation, as the fanship is now called by the papers, is not a democratic country (I mused as my running shoes got wet with the morning dew). Our ballplayers are black and white and Hispanic, but we're not. We're far too white, and we can somehow scrape together the outrageous sum of ninety dollars for a post-season seat.

The only things we are that might be termed "good" are devoted and fraternal. Some of us are Stephen-King rich, and some of us are still from Lowell—and probably should be saving the ninety clams for groceries. Some of us went to Phillips Andover, and some of us—me, my wife—went to Chelmsford High, and heard rumors of places like Phillips, just as Dad at Lowell High had heard the rumors, back when. Gail went to the same Catholic school, Notre Dame

Academy in Tyngsboro, that our mom went to long ago, and Gail once got invited to a party at Phillips and saw JFK Junior from across a crowded room. That's as close as kids from Chelmsford got.

But in the Nation, we all wear our B-hats the same way. We are one—hardly a democracy, but the best we can do. Those two eighty-year-old gents in chinos on the Phillips courts at seven forty-five on this brilliant Sunday morn. They're happily trading forehands, but they're dying that the Sox are now dead as doornails. Those two fifteen-year-old girls walking across the commons to chapel. They may be from Tennessee and Taiwan, but they're learning about the Nation, and if they're not yet citizens, they soon will be. Those young families down by the pond (as I jog back through the sanctuary), allowing their retrievers a frisky fall swim, they're discussing those babies that they bear in those Snugglies, no doubt, but they're also discussing the Red Sox collapse. Jim Powers, King of BLOHARDS, is lamenting—in Connecticut, probably, or maybe up here in Boston—the plight of the Bosox. Bill Lee lives in Vermont now, where he is sad this day. Dr. Jim Lonborg is sad on the Cape, and Carl Yastrzemski is sad down in Florida. My mom and brother in Chelmsford; my pals from childhood, Bruce, Mike, and Barry; Barry's parents on the Maine coast, Mike's mom in the old house on Middlesex Street, and Bruce's dad in the nursing home; Jane and Steve and Bo and John and the girls down in Larchmont, and Jane's parents in Wellesley (around the block from where my sister lives, having moved up from Chelmsford); the lobstermen on Isle au Haut, Maine; the loggers in Berlin, New Hampshire; the sociology professor at Middlebury in Vermont and the English prof at U-Conn; Roger Angell (and, yes, certainly: Roger could sue me for this particular gambit; is it plagiarism or am I sampling?), wherever Roger is—probably here, in Boston; my wife and my own kids back in Westchester, where this morning Caroline is crafting a note to leave for Daddy (a note I'll tell you about later) . . . my own dad in heaven above, up there with Ted . . . We're all dying that the Sox are dead, dead as doornails, and worst of all, dead at the hands of the Yankees. Again.

THE BAG AND I went to that 162nd ballgame in 1978 (and of course the 163rd), and we would go to the 169th of the 2004 season, regardless of what had happened the previous night.

"Who needs 'em?" the guy shouted. "Who needs two? Face value."

How the mighty had plunged. I had been told that I could get something like a twenty-six-fold profit for my ninety-dollar seats to the Angels—not the Yanks, the

Angels—and now this is what it had come to at 8:05 on Sunday evening. Later, between innings, the quiz on the message-board would ask us to guess the attendance. The answer would not be in the 35,000s, but, rather, the high 34s (i.e. some folks, so battered by the worst game ever, could not get to their feet. They wouldn't even show up).

I, however, had had a somewhat restorative afternoon. After my jog and Annie's marvelous breakfast of eggs and bacon, I'd driven over from Andover to visit with Mom and Kevin, and Gail had come out to Chelmsford, too. We'd watched the Patriots extend their winning streak to twenty, and, as we had done a hundred times in the last couple of years, we'd voiced our happiness that the Pats had "got it done" in Dad's lifetime—even if the Sox hadn't. (Footnote: That's not technically correct. The Red Sox did win the World Series in 1918, as we all know. Dad was, at the time, two.)

Brady had been customarily brilliant, and Gail and I had enjoyed the low-key visit. Then I was back in Andover, watching as Jake grilled steak. We ate in a leisurely fashion—we were in no hurry to get to the park—and then we four (Annie and daughter Maggie in back, Jake and I up front) headed down I-93 for the last game of the season. Lowe had been forced into service, so we were going to bid formal adieu to Derek—and, for that matter, Pedro, and surely that third-base coach who sends everyone, and whomsoever else was leaving the team tonight.

"Face value!" the guy shouted louder as he worked the parking lot opposite the ballpark. No takers.

Well, what to say about the next two games? That they were long? And dramatic? And went deep into extra innings? And featured two blown saves by Mariano? And traipsed upon early morning once, then serious nighttime on the same day as the aforesaid morning? History all over the place. The longest game in ALCS history (five hours and change on Sunday) followed by the longest game in post-season history (just shy of six hours on Monday). Twenty-eight innings of baseball, base runners all over the place—stranded, stranded, and stranded—climactic clouts, big steals, and runners thrown out, guys who beat out bunts and guys who couldn't bunt to save their lives.

What do you say about those games? Home runs by A-Rod and Papi and classy Bernie and all sorts of people in those games, lead changes, and . . . Do you say that Lowe, for whom we have a soft-spot because he threw his no-hitter while Dad was still alive, pitched great (and Francona pulled him too soon, thereby letting Timlin screw it up), or do you surge ahead to Dave Roberts' steal, and the crucial single by our Mariano foil, Bill Mueller, which tied it up in the ninth? Or to the witching-hour-plus performance by no-need-to-panic, you've-got-Lescanic? ("If you tell me Lescanic comes in tonight and wins," I said to Jake on the way out of the Sunday/Monday game, "I say to you, 'Well, then, it went twelve—and we'd already burned everyone else.'") What can I possibly say about the regal Ortiz? Can he do it every night? Apparently he can.

What do you say about the second of those games? Before answering, let's have Sheffield throw some fuel on the fire. "They're a walking disaster!" he said of our beloveds sometime in the wee hours of Monday morn. (He later said he didn't say it, but I think he said it.) Thank you, Gary, and we'll tack photocopies of that here and here and here in the locker room.

I don't know what to say about Pedro, in what I figured was his Sox swan song before becoming a Yankee. (Mets? Who knew?) Pedro pitched just as well as Lowe, that is until Francona allowed him to throw pitch one-hundred-and-one, which Jeter hit for a double, three runs scoring. So much going on all the time in this game! Do you even remember that Pedro then hit A-Rod (of course he did; his second hit batsman of the inning)? How about young Bronson's redemption that final night at the Fens, fanning Rodriguez and Sheffield? Sheffield misplaying Mientkiewicz's double? That's justice for you, fathead!

More to say! There's Varitek to talk about. He started the evening batting righty-on-righty against Mussina because he had done so dreadfully lefty-on-righty against him for years. Later, he flied to center off Rivera, tagging the "best closer of all time" with a second consecutive blown save for the first time in his career. (Sympathy's over, Mo.) 'Tek came up again with two outs and the winning run on second in the tenth, and I thought he was going to do it. He faced tired old Paul Quantrill, who'd given up the two-run shot to Papi in the twelfth the night before, and Jason, now comfortable on the southpaw side . . . popped up.

And so on to the eleventh! And two Sox pitchers (name 'em: Myers, Embree) struck out the side! And then Mueller singled and Bellhorn singled (after fanning at two bunt tries) . . . but it came to naught. The Sox couldn't buy a bunt—well, they never could, not since 1918—and Damon's series went even further south as he popped up his sacrifice try. The twelfth looked just like the previous night's twelfth—Manny followed by Ortiz—but this time they couldn't get it done, Ortiz robbed by an ump of his first post-season stolen base (but why was he running, anyway?).

How about Wakefield! How about Wake's thirteenth? A strikeout earned him a base runner, on the first of the inning's three passed balls. (Varitek never catches the knuckler in the regular season. Mirabelli does, and Jason showed why.) Finally, there were guys on second and third and Tim hadn't done a blessed thing wrong. (The walk had been intentional.) Wake fanned Sierra to end things but, whoa, that was weird. I was rooting for a pop-up rather than a K at the end, imagining a triumphant nanosecond following the punch-out, then a fourth PB and a loss. All of this is why we love baseball.

To the fourteenth we went, and Wake set 'em down one, two, three—Captain Jeter third.

And then . . .

I asked Jake subsequent to that fantastic bottom of the inning, "Was Ortiz's one of the ten—no, five—greatest at-bats you've ever seen live?"

"Easy."

"Top three?"

"I think so."

"Best?"

"Maybe. The thing is, everyone was so overwrought and exhausted and desperate at that point, you didn't think about that. It just seemed to go on forever."

Foul, foul, *ripped* foul, a . . . homer? . . . Noooo, foul. Foul. Foul. And then the hero broke his bat, the ball dropped into centerfield, *kerplop,* and Fenway was bedlam once more. Including the California game, three celebrations worthy of a pennant, all due to David (the third time, with an assist from Wake). As said, it's why we love the game.

My dear friend Jake had lived in Section 27 of Fenway Park for 17 of the last 54 hours on planet Earth; he had worked at his office six-to-eight (probably six). Of the remaining hours, he'd commuted three and slept in his Andover bed on a catch-as-catch-can basis. Of course there was the occasional half hour dedicated to nightcap, shower, or breakfast. The Bag was . . . well, he was tired, happy—and content to let the series return to New York.

We'll take it from here, good buddy.

BACK IN THE Empire State, it was nothing like a homecoming (except for the warm embrace of my family). On Tuesday, I donned my Sox cap and headed to the train for the ride to Grand Central. Although Yankee fans were getting nervous and therefore ugly, I had to wear the cap to work. Our twins were wearing their Red Sox T-shirts to Jennie's School for Little Children, Caroline was wearing her B-hat to second grade. Would Daddy chicken out? He would not. How could he, when Caroline was sticking up for the Sox even against the imposing Sister Margaret at CCD class? I'd learned from Wendy, our Mary Poppins of a nanny, that Sister Margaret had given Caroline grief over her Sox garb. Apparently the priests and nuns of Saint John's and Saint Mary's were trying to enforce some sort of pro-Yankee fiat within the flock, just like those bishops out West were coercing Bush-backing in the election. But even

Sister Margaret could not bully a four-year-old. When Wendy arrived to pick up Caroline, and Sister Margaret brought up the subject, Mary Grace looked her square in the eye and declared, "Red Sox win." The simplicity and innocence of the child left the old girl dumbstruck. Sister Margaret, good Catholic that she was, knew Truth when she heard it. The Red Sox were winning, in a fashion and now, suddenly, at a pace that was messing with New York's head.

The stadium on a raw Tuesday night was entirely different than it had been a week earlier. It was not festive, it was on edge. And Curt Schilling was wholly different than he had been a week earlier, too. He was on a mission. I wondered, subsequently, what Sister Margaret thought about Curt's insistence that God had carried him and his dicey tendon through the seven innings. I never credit that stuff—hey, Mariano's a real minister, and he'd just blown two saves—but on that Tuesday night I was thinking, *Whatever works.*

Something carried Schilling, there's no question about that. Something bore him up. He was huge, and he was floating above the ground. It was one of the most impressive starting performances I've ever witnessed. The reason I say so: The Yankee fans looked upon it, and knew what they were seeing. They were silenced from the get-go. Curt, as he had said he hoped to, was shutting them up. I swear, by the fourth or fifth, Yankee Stadium seemed to sense there would be a Game Seven.

*Where did the bats go?* the Stadium asked as one. The top of the Yanks order—one through four—which could not make an out in the first three games, now suffered its third straight night of ineffectiveness. Go figure. A-Rod looked nervous. Matsui looked like a rookie. It was all very strange. The Sox, as well, were curious to look at in Game Six. After five frames, Mueller (hitting in the two-spot) Ramirez and Ortiz were oh-for-eight, and we were ahead four-to-oh. Everyone below the equator in our lineup seemed to be two-for-two, and the guy who wasn't, Bellhorn, had just jacked a three-run dinger. That was the kind of Red Sox team that was going to win games.

The Bellhorn homer delivers us crisply to the subject of umpires. I was gleeful at the way Game Six transpired. There's nothing better that having umps overturn calls to get them right, then have Yankee fans feel they've been wronged. Jobbed. Cheated.

Let's face it, Bellhorn cranked it out, and A-Rod did a dirty deed. All of Mr. Torre's later mumbling about something else going on during the A-Rod play was baloney. His star third baseman, who the *Times* was kind enough to point out the next day had been "anemic all season in clutch situations," got caught out. He slapped that ball, just like a bush leaguer might.

While we're on the subject: Call me a conspiracy theorist, but I can't believe instant replay doesn't already exist in post-season baseball. The umps got their two overturns precisely correct, but this phenomenon of the umpire huddle, with the sixth ump jogging in late (with news as to how the replay and commentary looked on national television, perhaps?) is a new-millennium thing—as are the smart overturns themselves. What I'm saying is, ten years ago neither Bellhorn's homer nor A-Rod's dastardliness would have been set right. And you know what I think of the New World Order? I like it.

The Yankee fans did not. In the stands, the thugs got thuggish, and suddenly SWAT troops in riot gear lined the field. *Ah, this is where I live. The national pastime, New York style.* I was wondering to myself what Professor McCarver's commentary was just then. Foul-ball interference on the part of a law-enforcement officer was no doubt being limned.

Game One was a wild one, Game Two was classic baseball, Game Three was a stinker (or a rout, if you're from the other side), Games Four and Five were otherworldly, and Game Six was, again, classic baseball (with the weird footnote of the overturns). Schilling was a hero, a maligned player (Bellhorn) stepped up, and Keith Foulke was a second hero. He was now Mariano. You could feel it. The Stadium was so tense when he walked those two in the ninth, because everyone there was aware of one salient fact: Foulke knows how to close. In years past, Yanks fans could readily assume that those walks were coming home and somewhere John Sterling was about to bleat into his microphone, *"Thhhhhhuuuuu Yankees Win!!"* No longer. Not with Foulke.

And then, Game Seven—and deliverance.

I met my seat mate, Mike Padden again, at the middle flag pole near the Big Bat, as is our New York custom, and we proceeded to climb way, way up into the reaches of the stadium whence the bottles flew the night before. Mike avers that I'm the one hardcore Sox fan he can bear to watch a Yanks-Sox game with and, ultimately, I feel the same way about him (though I still consider him a despicable traitor). Even in nail-biting time, we behave with consideration for one another, and that is requisite. For Game Seven, with Luci declining—"Not again, not this year"— Mike got the call.

The atmosphere was something approaching electric, but it wasn't electric. There was a large measure of desperation in the air, and the least sense of foreboding. Kevin Brown was to start, and any astute Yankee fan not only begrudged him the wall-punching incident, but knew that, despite a couple of pretty fair outings against other teams since coming off the DL, he had been severely roughed-up twice by the Red Sox—including once in this series. The fourth inning against the Sox was looking like the Promised Land, to him.

It was believed Wakefield would be Boston's starter, but there was D. Lowe scribbled in on game day. Based on what they had done in the very recent past, either pitcher was deserving. Here were two veteran Sox who had had poor-to-fair seasons but were coming up big in show time. Everyone kept saying Lowe was pitching for a contract, but that had been true all year. You get to start Game Seven against the Yankees, you try to bring your best, I figured, whether you are signed or floating free.

The Sox—Ortiz again, with a smash to right—staked Lowe to a 2-0 lead. Brown was lucky he didn't give up more; he looked just as bad as he he'd routinely looked against the Sox that autumn. Lowe, by contrast, looked silky smooth. He was as good as he'd been all year. He was throwing grounders, and so was clearly on form.

It wasn't the best of games, but it was precisely what was needed. Damon came alive with that grand slam after Brown departed in the second. Lowe threw sixty-nine pitches through six before Francona did the absolutely unthinkable. He brought in Pedro, thereby ushering a desultory crowd back into the game *("Who's your Daddy!?!?!?")*. High in the upper deck, I began to sweat.

And looking around, I realized I wasn't alone in my anxiety. The prospective blowout (8-1 when Pedro arrived) had caused the more edgy of the Yankee fans to vent their frustrations—usually upon Red Sox fans. Up and down, up and down went the cops, carting out drunks. Something strange was happening as a consequence. With the upper deck pruned, Red Sox fans became a more prominent presence. Little groups formed. One merry band even tried a rhythmic "Let's Go Red Sox!" cheer.

Hey, we all know what happened in the game; the lead was so large, Pedro's mucking around wouldn't—couldn't—turn this into a reprise of the Disaster of '03. And we all know that the series win was both the biggest comeback and the biggest collapse in sports history—no one had ever prevailed from oh-three down in baseball. And we all know that it all ended on Mickey Mantle's birthday. We all know all of that.

There's little I can tell you that might be new. I can only begin to conjure the giddy surreality of it all. Yankee Stadium a half hour after the final pitch was one of the most bizarre places I've ever been. There was no one in the arena except the considerable contingent of Red Sox rooters. We were all high-fiving one another, and posing for pictures with the scrum of happy Red Sox down on the field in the background. Everyone was smiling. Sinatra's "New York, New York," was blaring over and over and over on the loudspeakers, and no one heard it. We owned the Yankees that night, and we owned Yankee Stadium. It was a very strange thing. We had got it done—that far, at least. Those guys, at least. And we could hardly believe it.

I called Luci from the Stadium of course, and Gail, and Mom. My mother talked about how she'd seen most of it, and how excited she was. Dad was left unsaid. I reflected silently to myself (as Mom went to summon Kevin to the phone) that the best World Series game I'd even seen had been with my mother—and it'd been a Red Sox loss. In 1986 we had got off to a searing start at Shea, and of course I had asked Dad if he wanted to go to Game Three in Fenway. Even that long ago, he'd felt Boston and all the game-day excitement might be a bit much for him. "Take your mother," he'd said, perhaps being earnest about his own condition, perhaps just wanting me to take my mother.

I drove into town, dropped her off in front of the Ritz, and parked the car under the Common. I hustled back to the hotel, and sat with my mom in the world's greatest bar for an hour. She nursed a whiskey sour, and I played Dad, ordering a Beefeater martini. The sun set as we looked out through those marvelous windows on that marvelous tableau that is the Public Gardens. I paid the tab with a credit card (Dad never had a credit card, his whole life). Mom and I walked slowly across the street afterwards, and watched the Swan Boats shut down for the evening. I grabbed a cab, and it took us as close as it could—the southwestern tip of the Cask and Flagon. (Today, they can't get nearer than Kenmore.) We walked towards our gate, and Mom stopped to buy—and enjoy—a sausage sandwich. The sauce dripped, and stained her sweater. As I cleaned it I noticed she was wearing a pin—what do they call it? A brooch?—that I'd bought her when I was in college, and had about fifty bucks each December to shell out on about ten presents for various friends and family. I'm sure I got it at Marshalls or T.J.'s. It was paste, but she had thought to wear it.

We took our seats in right field that night, and watched the Sox lose to the Mets, a precursor of far, far more dramatic events to come. It was one of the four or five, maybe even two or three, best games of my life.

"Mom," I said simply when I called her from Yankee Stadium, "We did it."

She said the same thing she always said, but it was a thing that she always meant honestly: "Isn't it something." It was declarative. No question mark.

"Congratulations, Sull," Mike said after I'd finished my phone calls. "Let me take your picture."

As I leaned on the upper-deck railing and smiled, the Bosox still partying behind me, I put my hands in the pockets of my slacks. In the left pocket was my wallet—familiar—and in the right were my keys and a piece of paper. After Mike snapped a photo, I withdrew the crumpled note.

Now, I've mentioned earlier that Caroline had written me a message of consolation at one point. After the Sox had dropped the first three games of what would become The Greatest Series Ever Played, she had composed a sweet missive to Daddy. After I had returned from Boston and grabbed an hour's sleep, I had come downstairs to find the scrap next to my coffee mug.

new york yankees stink.

red sox rock!!

Yeah!

Dear DaD

Happy Birthday

From Caroline

I'd been carrying it around all week, and I looked at it anew in Yankee Stadium. What I found poignant was, we were nowhere near my birthday. But kids know what cheers a person up. And Caroline had known that Daddy needed cheering up. I'm being honest. That note did as much for me—no, it did more—than what the Red Sox wound up doing in that phenomenal, ferocious series. Which was plenty.

The note, as I read it at Yankee Stadium for a hundredth time, made me lament that I hadn't spent more time with Caroline, Jack, and Mary Grace that week. I resolved then and there to watch the World Series from home.

And I couldn't wait to see the kids at the breakfast table the next morning, and tell them who'd won.

"IT MEANS NOT rubbing it in."

I was explaining to them, on the morning after the seventh game, what "gloating" means, and also "goading"—and why these were two things the Sullivan children were not to do on this day. They were new words for the kids, and Caroline, as team leader, had asked for a parsing.

"Particularly with Reed," I continued as the kids munched their Cheerios thoughtfully. Reed would be at the bus stop in a half-hour's time unless he had killed himself, and I wasn't going to have Caroline lighting into Reed. "Reed takes the Yankees seriously, so he'll be having a rough day. I'm going to be nice to Mr. Stanski on the train, and I want you to be nice to Reed on the bus."

"Okay," Caroline said. "Can I wear my B-hat."

"Sure," I said, taking note that Wendy had already issued Jack his Bosox T-shirt for use on that glorious day. "It's okay to wear stuff, and it's okay to be happy. Just don't brag, and don't rub it in. We're going to take the high road."

"To where?" Jack asked.

"It's an expression."

"What's that mean?" asked Caroline. "What's an expression?" I was still befogged by my delirious experience at the Stadium the night before, and was obviously struggling with breakfast.

"It means," I said, "we're going to be classy."

"What's that mean?" asked Jack. "Like Mrs. D'Agostino's class?" Mary Grace was letting her brother lead. She was happy that the Sox had won because it made Daddy happy, but she didn't really seem to care what any of this meant.

"When do the Red Sox play again?" Caroline asked.

"Saturday night. Against either the Cardinals or the Astros." Jack perked up at that word. The girls had no reaction. If it wasn't the Sox playing the hated Yankees, it mattered little to them.

And, interestingly, their old man was having similar feelings in the immediate aftermath of the Greatest Series Ever Played. Our boy wonder GM probably expressed it best for Red Sox Nation when he said, after getting by the Yanks, "Now we have to beat Finland." That was about right. You might remember that the 1980 United States gold-medal ice hockey team beat Finland to win the Olympic tournament, and then again you might not. But you sure remember that, earlier, they beat the Russkies.

We had beaten our Russkies.

"Are you going to the game on Saturday?" Caroline asked. There was something in her voice that implied she preferred I not fly off to Boston yet again, and I was happy to tell her, "No. I'll stay and watch with you."

Which is exactly what I did. We had all this family stuff to attend to—parties, parades, soccer games. I wasn't going to go chasing another baseball series, no matter how consequential it was. I'm a huge fan, but I'm also a family man. My latest plan, a slight variation on my intentions on the eve of the ALCS, was to watch an inning or two with Caroline, maybe as many as six or seven with Luci, then take in whatever excruciating endings were in store by my lonesome (with my sister always available on the other end of the cell phone line, just as Dad had once been).

As I walked down the hill to the train station on the morning after Game Seven, I tried to come to terms with who I wanted to join us at the dance, Houston or St. Louis. I found two compelling factors for either. With Houston you had the fun of facing Clemens, and of course, cosmically, there was a whole Massachusetts-Texas fooforah right then with the election. St. Louis, for its part, was legendarily the world's best baseball town with the world's best fans, and also, two of the last four Sox World Series, '46 and '67, had been lost in seven exciting games to the Redbirds. This was about baseball, not politics, and so I developed a rooting interest for the Cards in their impending decisive game against the 'stros. The Sox going through California, New York, and St. Louis to win this fateful championship. That, I decided, was a proper way to do it.

I was extremely gentle with Mr. Stanski—Stan—on the train ride to Gotham. The entire fifty-two minutes were spent talking baseball, of course, and we pretty much stuck to the technical details and what Steinbrenner's wrath might now mean for assorted coaches and how Kevin Brown was a chump (no argument there) and how . . .

Only once did I veer perilously close to mean-spirited-ness. "Stan," I said, "How do Yanks fans feel about A-Rod at the end of Year One?"

"I think he's the best player in the game," answered Stan.

Okay. Fine. New topic.

Stan and I survived the commute with our friendship intact, and I made my way through the labyrinthine tunnels of Grand Central's Northwest Passage to the Madison Avenue sidewalk. In the five city blocks that I walked to the office, four or five people yelled or quietly offered congratulations and wishes of "good luck." (They were reacting to my cap.) One woman, trailing me, shouted something like, "Yeeee-ahhhh!" The two folks in front of me turned with a start, thinking someone was being mugged or murdered. They looked around in a darting fashion, saw nothing that they either did or did not want to get involved in, and then proceeded on their way.

That night I rooted home the Cards over the Astros. (I did get a soupçon of delight seeing Fatass Clemens go down.) Then I began putting on my game face. Next morning, I went to the city similarly accoutered as on the day after the Day. I received a different reception. "Take off the damned hat!" This was issued by someone on the other side of the street. That evening, "Boston sucks." All goodwill was gone, and I realized, *I'm gloating.* Yesterday, we were still in the event, and Yankee fans were passing a torch. This day, I was wearing a hat indoors, in someone else's house. It was impolite. I would, I then resolved, only wear the B-hat during the games. (And maybe at breakfast after a win.)

What was my favorite sporting event on that first Saturday of the Series? Caroline's soccer game, swear to God. I had encouraged her to show a little more spark when getting to the ball—she's a fast runner, but would slow down when she came into proximity of heavy action—and, sure enough, she enjoyed a couple of breakaways. After the match, she was so delighted with her progress that she wanted to practice one-on-one with Daddy for twenty more minutes. The day was cool and gray, the foliage enclosing the field was stunning (was it coincidence or providence that the glorious Autumn of the Red Sox was also the most beautiful in the Northeast's recent memory?) and the twenty minutes were, for Dad, as good as it gets. Was I glad I wasn't running off to catch the four-thirty Delta Shuttle? I honestly was.

The agreement with Caroline was that if she chilled in her room while we put the twins to bed, she could come downstairs and watch some baseball. That was a treat for her dad, too. She snuggled between Luci and me, and set off on a series of intelligent questions. "Did the Cardinals beat the Yankees, too?" "Is Aunt Gail there?" "Why do you get scared, Daddy, every time he throws."

Well, the "he" was good old Wakefield, and that's enough said. I loved Wakefield as a brother—there's no finer human being on the team, and he's as gutsy as they come in the sport of baseball, and his various contributions against the Yanks had been heroic in all sorts of ways—but he offered a flutterball, and despite his work against New York, he had been going poorly of late.

My fears proved well founded. Though given an early lead, Wake was not long for that night. Neither was Caroline, who started to nod in the fifth. I promised that I would rouse her with the news if the Sox won—a promise I would later break, just as I had broken the Game Seven promise in 2003—and then I gave my eldest a kiss good-night. She and Luci departed for bed, and I was left with the agony of watching four errors committed and a lead blown before Bellhorn—Bellhorn!—did it again.

Sunday morning after Mass we gave Sister Margaret a good-natured hard time, and she responded by declaring, "I will not pray for your Red Sox." (The good nun refrained from calling them "your g-d Red Sox.")

"They don't need it," I responded, then wondered at my cockiness. Since when are Bosox fans possessed of any small measure of bravado, be it fact-based or false? I'll tell you since when. Since our team hooked up fifty-two times in two seasons with the mega-million-buck Yankees, each and every go-round a playoff-intensity fray, and split that enormous series right down the middle—now, even unto one ALCS title apiece. It's like boning a bat. If a two-season experience like that—a season unto itself, encased within the larger seasons—doesn't make a team ready to beat any and everybody else, then nothing will, not for another eighty-six years.

Sunday afternoon saw our merry band attend a ragamuffin parade downtown, then a private Halloween party. Caroline was a witch (figuratively), Mary Grace was Dorothy (from The Wizard of Oz; not the Wiggles' dinosaur), and Jack was, inevitably, Spider-Man—one of perhaps fifty Spider-Men in the parade. Mommy was well-dressed as usual—she refuses at all times to make an idiot of herself—and Daddy, gleefully an idiot most days but at Holloween with license, was a cowboy. I donned the Akubra, the Driza-bone coat, the pointy-toed boots, the denim shirt, the belt with the big buckle, and the string tie from some insipid theme party in the '80s—the precise same get-up I wore for a week straight in October of 2003. Was I jinxing the '04 club by taking Cowboy Up! out of the closet? Ha. If I was feeling tough enough to face down Sister Margaret, I could take on any remnants of the Curse.

The Stanskis were at the parade and Stan gave me a bit of grief about how poorly the Sox had played in Game One. I didn't take the bait. My club was in, his was out. I had told Luci that morning, though, "That game was close, but nothing like Four and Five last week. The difference was those were great games. Last night's stunk." It truly had. But you know what? It was a win, and it was a win in the Wakefield game. It was a win in the Wakefield game in the World Series, a thing you're not readily giving back.

During a party after the parade, I was at the bar with three Jets fans when Pennington scored with a minute and forty-eight seconds left in the first half. I casually remarked, "They've left Brady too much time." Which they had, and the score would remain frozen at 13-6, Pats in front, till the game's final gun. I was turning into one pretty smartass sports fan. I knew everything. The way I figured it at that moment in time, the Sox were going to sweep.

Sunday night I watched the whole thing alone, as it was a school night and Luci was beat from all of the weekend activity. Four more errors but, whoa, that Schilling. This was even gutsier than what he had done against the Yanks, because this night, he didn't have his stuff. That's the way, FOX: Go to the sock again. Show me the sock. *Gimme that bloody sock.*

I started wondering, during that game, about the truisms surrounding this Cardinals team. Truisms: St. Louis was the best hitting team in baseball. St. Louis was the best clutch-hitting team in baseball. St. Louis was the best team in baseball on the base paths. Rolens and Pujols were RBI machines.

So, then, we would hang our hopes on creaming St. Louis's suspect starting pitching, right? That seemed like a good strategy, and the way to go about executing such a strategy might be to score first-inning runs. And, through Game Two, the attack plan was working fine.

But those truisms again. Guess what? Turned out we were the best clutch-hitting team in baseball. Clearly the idea against the Cards' starters was patience—get your pitch—and only a week after deciding that Matsui was the best two-strike hitter I'd ever seen, I amended that opinion to: any current Red Sox is the best two-strike hitter I've ever seen and our entire team is the best two-out-hitting team I've ever seen. St. Louis pitchers seemed to be living the proverbial one strike away, and then, snatch, it was gone, and the ball was floating towards a gap or towards the bleachers. People named Bellhorn (yet again!) and Cabrera were doing this to them, while big lugs named Pujols and Rolens and Edwards were doing nada. Interesting.

Of all of the stats that I saw in the paper on the commuter-train ride Monday morning, the one that struck me was this: of 350-something pitches delivered to the Sox in Games One and Two, the batters had swung cleanly through 18. The guys simply weren't missing anything.

My friend, Jane, had attended the first two. I called her once she had returned to New York on the shuttle, and wasn't surprised by her report. "It was great . . . of course it was really great . . . But, you know, it wasn't near as intense as last week. I don't know if it's the girl getting killed or post-Yankee letdown or what. But it really was weird. The team was winning the World Series, and at no time was it like last week."

Jane had mentioned what most Sox fans were leaving unsaid in those climactic days. The girl getting killed. After the seventh game of the Yanks series, 80,000 had packed in and around Kenmore Square, and some of the kids started going nuts. Cops began shooting pepper spray at them and, apparently, a young woman from Emerson College caught some square in the eye. She died. It was an appalling, heartbreaking tragedy, and certainly it would cast a gloom over the World Series for any thinking fan. It also left us all praying—all of us, Sister Margaret included—that if the Sox won this thing, Boston would stay peaceful.

The stands in St. Louis were rocking and rolling before the first pitch of Game Three, so there was only one thing to do—score in the first inning again, and shut them up. I think when Suppan got caught off third by our nimble first baseman Ortiz, Cards fans knew the universe was out of whack and they might not be coming back in this series. Their boppers weren't bopping, their base runners were blundering and the Sox were starting to look positively slick. Manny was hitting like David, David was fielding like Pujols, Pedro was drawing a walk, and Rolens was hitting like Pedro. Most important, Pedro was slinging like old Pedro, and that's a pitcher who can win you a big game. Which he did.

So there we sat, after three games, having led every single one of the twenty-seven innings of the World Series (meaning, you win 'em all). And there I sat that final night, in front of the tube, firmly believing we, behind Derek, were about to get it done.

The feeling was universal in Red Sox Nation. I had been receiving confident e-mails all day long, from BLO-HARDS and others. Bruce, Mike, and Barry had sent proclamations from Massachusetts and Rhode Island. John had checked in from Providence as well. (Yankee fan)

Mike and (Met fan) Art had sent along best wishes from Brooklyn and New Jersey, respectively. Pat (no relation) Sullivan, once of New Hampshire, had gotten in touch from Kauai, Hawaii, where he lives with his family and roots home his Bosox over brunch.

One message arrived only moments before the first pitch of Game Four. The Bag sent an email headlined "AT THE RISK OF"—an allusion to jinxing what was about to transpire in Missouri. All you need to know to decipher it is that Tom was Jake's dad and Hampton is a beach in New Hampshire where families from Lowell used to vacation. Maybe still do.

The email read:

> I just know that a few short hours from now, your
> father, my dad, and countless others who never had
> the good fortune to experience here on earth the ulti-
> mate sports fan's pleasure, but who ushered their sons
> and daughters into the Sox fellowship, will be setting
> up their lounge chairs in heaven's family room, beam-
> ing in anticipation of the pleasure of finally seeing
> baseball's version of the Holy Grail in our communal
> grasp. Ted, Tony C., Harry Agganis, Joe Cronin,
> Smoky Joe Wood, Ned Martin, Ken Coleman, and
> countless others, large and small, famous and other-
> wise, will also be in the house for the occasion.*

Even they don't know the exact score, or in which game, they do know that this time, at long last, they'll soon be pounding each other on the back and smiling down on us here below as we exult for our team, ourselves, our own next generation of fans, and for them.

I'd also like to think that Tom and Artie are right now reminiscing together about one almost-forgotten summer at Hampton—yet another lost campaign for the Sox—and thinking how the ironies abound that each had a son—and fellow Sox fanatic—who years later renewed their acquaintance, went on to share a college experience that can't be duplicated, an eternal friendship (and one even introduced the other to the love of his life)—and albeit with lengthy intervals of years in between, continued to go together to countless Sox games, both humdrum and historic.

> Long may we run.
> Jake

* They're not sure whether the Babe will be there, even though everybody invited him. They're not sure because it's not completely clear that he'd be unambiguously happy to be amongst them for that purpose, and also because, as usual, he's got plans to roister at numerous other parties.

Now we know the exact score. Now we know the Cards never woke up. Now we know they never touched our starting pitching, post-Wake. Now we know that Boston stayed relatively peaceful on that fairy-dusted night. Now we know that ours is the seventh team ever to win the World Series after being three outs away from elimination, the fourth never to trail in the Series, and the first to win eight in a row in the post-season. Now we know the lunar eclipse aided and abetted a re-ordering of the universe. Now we know God is not necessarily a Yankee fan. Now we know the Red Sox got it done in our lifetimes—and will get it done again.

Yes, they will.

They did it six times for Fred Hale.

I will explain.

THERE WAS, FOR ME, a postscript chapter to the great triumph, as I'm sure there was for all of us, each fan's PS a little different than another's. Mine included hugs with the kids and wife, and champagne all around (well, not for the four-year-olds). The World Series was over so fast (it would take a while to sink in, what a truly bad series it had been), that we had time to set aside Saturday night for our small family celebration. "Here's to the Red Sox," I said, raising a glass.

"Here's to us," said Luci.

A little later, also part of the personal postscript, was

that BLOHARDS function referenced at the very beginning of this narrative—the party at the Yale Club with Jane at which we gazed upon the World Championship trophy. A third part of my addendum included an early Christmas present from Luci's sister, who sent a Waterford crystal commemorative baseball that now sits on my desk atop a piece-of-the-old-left-field-wall paperweight that Dad bought me back in . . . let me see here . . . back in 1976. Interestingly, partial proceeds from the paperweight and the crystal went, twenty-eight years apart, to the Jimmy Fund. (Hey, Ted, they benefited the little kids with cancer.)

Lastly, my own postscript also included one final trip to Beantown.

The magazine for which I work was one of several that wanted to put Curt Schilling on the cover of a December issue. At our general-interest periodical, there was serious concern that no one in the photo department knew how to "talk baseball." My colleagues realized, as you might guess, that I was fluent, and so I was dispatched to Boston to try and keep Curt happy, perhaps thereby stretching a fifteen-minute cover-shoot to a half-hour.

I flew up, then drove out from Logan through the Ted Williams Tunnel. I steered southwest to Medfield, to the large, gated property that Schilling bought from Bledsoe upon joining the Sox. As I piloted my Hertz rental, I reflected that this was the very route that Curt had driven in the opposite direction—all these tree-lined New England back roads—on that morning of his World Series win. His ankle tendon, frayed beyond repair and stitched to his skin in hopes that the jerry-built solution might hold, had been aching something terrible, and Curt was sure he would have to scratch as a starter.

But then he had started seeing the signs: GO CURT! THIS IS THE YEAR. WE LOVE YOU, CURT. Every quarter mile had brought a new sign—GOD BLESS YOU, CURT!—and by the time he'd reached Fenway, he was ready to lace up.

The radio was transporting me back. I had put on 'BCN for old times' sake, and a cover of "Just Another Brick In the Wall" by Korn was followed by the original of "London Calling" by the Clash. Songs I had heard, on so many trips to Fenway.

I shook hands with Schilling, engaged in small talk, asked him how the surgery had gone and how long he might be wearing the cast. I said hello to his wife. It was all very nice. He was obviously tired, but gave us plenty of time; we got our picture. During the shoot itself, I wandered about the foyer, looking at the pictures of Curt and his kids. I kept circling back to ask him a Hot Stove question, trying to keep him engaged and on our side.

"Who was the last Red Sox on LIFE's cover?" Curt asked.

"The only two," I answered, "were Ted and Yaz."

"Wow," he said. Schilling has an ego as large as his physique, as ball fans know, but he sounded earnest. He is—like Clemens is—a big kid at heart. He and Clemens, the biggest kids in the playground

Forty-five minutes after the first click of the camera, I thanked Schilling for his hospitality and time. No, I was not going to ask him for an autograph for my kids—I'm a professional—but to my considerable surprise, I then thanked Schilling for joining "our" team. I thanked him for what he had done. And then I said, "My dad would've gotten a huge kick out of it." I added, "You were his kind of player."

*Why'd I need to say that?* What does he care? I'm a pro, a fifty-one-year-old journalist. *Why'd I say that?*

"That's nice to hear," said Schilling, gently letting me off the hook.

When I was driving back to Logan, a Christmas song came on 'BCN, "Merry, Merry, Merry Freakin' Christmas" by the Freakin' A's. It was all about the Sox beating the Yanks. The Freakin' A's were, apparently, a garage band looking to make a buck on the back of the Sox' success. They weren't even from Boston, they were from Cincinnati. Kind of a latter-day Standells: ersatz Beantowners. They were backpackers, is what they were.

Fred Hale was no backpacker. I heard on the news that he had died in his sleep in suburban Syracuse on November

19. At the time he was twelve days shy of his 114th birthday, the world's oldest known man. Mr. Hale was a lifelong Boston Red Sox fan, and had lived to see them win it again—adding to '03, '12, '15, '16 and '18. Six championships. There's hope for us all. How many more might they win for me and Luci, Gail and Scott, Kevin, Jake and Annie, Mike, Bruce, and Barry—all the others. How about another or two or three for Mom? How many might they eventually win for Caroline, Jack, and Mary Grace?

That was one reflection. Another was, *Mr. Hale, meet Dad. Meet Ted. Meet Tom Lamond and Jack Kilmartin and Reggie Larkin and . . .*

A final notion was, *Nineteen-eighteen certainly was a long time ago.*

Two thousand and four, however . . . it seems like only yesterday.